Contents

APPLYING FOR A JOB

The Essential Guide

Need
— 2 —
Know

Sasa
Jankovic

First published in Great Britain in 2010 by
Need2Know
Remus House
Coltsfoot Drive
Peterborough
PE2 9JX
Telephone 01733 898103
Fax 01733 313524
www.need2knowbooks.co.uk

Need2Know is an imprint of Forward Press Ltd.
www.forwardpress.co.uk
SB ISBN 978-1-86144-099-0
Cover photograph: Dreamstime

Introduction

Whether it's your first or your 31st, applying for a job can seem like a daunting task.

Deciding what kind of work you would like to do is hard enough, but then you have to work out if you have the skills, qualifications and experience you need. And that's the easy part – next you have to contend with writing your CV and covering letter, submitting an application form, working out what to include (and what to leave out), preparing yourself for going to an interview or, if it doesn't work out, dealing with a rejection.

All of this is simply part of the process of selling yourself to prospective employers, and it doesn't have to be difficult. In fact, there are plenty of ways to make it a relatively straightforward process. This book is full of good advice and insider tips about how you can find the job you want, put together a professional application and create the right impression at interview.

It will also tell you what to do if you are offered the job, and how to handle rejection if things don't turn out as you hope, as well as what to do if you are applying for your first job, and how to return to the world of work if you have had a career break or want to change direction.

'It is never too late – or too early – to take the right steps on the path to the career you've always wanted.'

Although you'll never get a second chance to make a good first impression, it is never too late – or too early – to take the right steps on the path to the career you've always wanted. And while we can't guarantee that reading this book will help you get every job you apply for, it will certainly give you a head start when it comes to getting the attention of prospective employers.

Good luck, and happy job hunting.

Chapter One

Looking for a Job

What do you want to do?

Deciding what you want to do is half the battle when it comes to looking for a job. However, while you should try to have the attitude that nothing is out of your reach, it is important to be realistic. There is probably not much call for lion tamers, for example, but there are plenty of companies looking for people with a good level of computer skills.

List your passions

Begin by imagining what your dream job would be, and write a list of your passions. Maybe you've always wanted to work with children, or you love books and libraries, or you get real satisfaction from helping people. Perhaps you've always known that you want to be a nurse, or a firefighter, or a marine biologist. If you have the choice and the chance to do a job that you are truly passionate about then you are more likely to enjoy it and do it well. Be honest with yourself about what you really want to do.

Be realistic

Honesty is a good starting point, but you have to be realistic as well. If you were to ask any successful business person how they got to the top of their chosen profession, they would all probably tell you that they started at the bottom and worked their way up. You can't expect to walk straight into the job of your dreams from day one.

'Nothing is out of your reach, but it is important to be realistic.'

Say you love hill walking and the great outdoors, and your ideal job would be as a professional mountain guide. If you've never worked as a mountain guide before then it is unrealistic to expect that you would be chosen for such a position straightaway if you applied for it. What is more likely is that you would have to start at the bottom – say, working in a specialist outdoor clothing and equipment shop, or as some kind of assistant in an outdoor visitor centre – and work your way up.

Skills and experience

Once you have an idea of what you really want to do, make another list of all the skills and experience you have so you can clearly see what matches up with the requirements of the kind of job you want, and what gaps there are.

'Make a list of the skills and experience you have so you can clearly see what matches up with the requirements of the kind of job you want.'

If you want to be a nurse then you will need certain qualifications. If you want to be a firefighter then you will also need special training, will have to be physically fit and probably not afraid of heights. If you want to be a lion tamer, it is probably best that you are not allergic to cats!

When you are starting out on your career path, or even choosing a new one, no one expects you to have all the skills and experience that you are going to need right from the start.

Transferable skills

Let's say that you are really interested in property development and want to work in an estate agent's office, but have never done so before. This doesn't have to mean that you won't be able to get a job there. Everyone has to start somewhere, and the way in is to be able to convince a potential employer that you have a good basic level of skills that would enable you to begin to do the kind of work they do. These are called 'transferable skills'.

So, using the estate agent's office job as an example, think about the kind of transferable skills you have that would be attractive to this kind of employer. Are you good with numbers? Perhaps you have previous experience of dealing with customers on the telephone? Do you already have any qualifications that might be of use – a driving licence, GCSE or O-Level maths, or even good typing skills.

If you think there are gaps in your skills that would prevent you from getting the kind of job you want, talk to other people who already do that sort of work. Ask for their advice about what other skills you might need to boost your chances of getting a job in that particular field.

The government's website Careers Advice Direct is a good place to start for advice on courses, careers and learning (see help list).

There will also be various associations and professional bodies connected with whatever field you are looking to work in, and it is worth getting in touch with them for more information. The Alliance of Sector Skills Councils (see help list) brings together all 25 licensed UK Sector Skills Councils, and you can search on their website to find out what skills you need to do certain jobs.

Who do you want to work for and why?

Once you know what you want to do, you need to decide which company you want to work for and why.

This is a very important part of the process of applying for a job, as it is the main reason a company will select someone for interview. When you send in your job application – and go for an interview if you are selected – you must be able to make it very clear why you want to work for this particular company above any other.

So, in order to convince them, you have to be convinced yourself. Reasons for wanting to work for a particular organisation might include:

- They are the best in their field.
- They offer plenty of training.
- They win awards for their work.
- They are well known as an ethical organisation.
- They have green credentials, which are important to you.
- You particularly admire the work of one of their employees or departments.

'When you send in your job application, you must be able to make it very clear why you want to work for this particular company above any other.'

For example, say you really want to be a graphic designer. You hear that Glow Design Ltd and TW Creative Studios are both advertising jobs that you think you could do. Glow Design is really close to where you live, and one of your friends work there too, but you know that the company doesn't offer any training to new staff. You think you would prefer to work at TW Creative Studios, which is an hour's train journey away but has won some industry awards and is well known for offering a lot of staff training and promoting its employees.

When you apply for the job at TW Creative Studios, you need to mention in your application why you particularly want to work for them. Then if you are selected for interview, you must again be prepared to make your reasons very clear, and state them in a positive way. We will talk more about interview techniques and how to answer these kinds of questions in chapter 5 but, for now, you will find it useful to practise thinking how you can justify your choices.

How to plan job hunting

The thought of looking for a job can be pretty daunting, so the best way to approach it, in order to not get bogged down, is to plan out your job hunting strategy. In effect, treat job hunting as if it is your job.

If you are not working at the moment then you will probably have some blocks of free time that you can use for job hunting. If you currently have a job then you will have to fit your job searching around your work, which can take a bit more planning but is not impossible. Set aside a few hours each week to focus on searching out job vacancies and sending in your applications, and stick to it. Some people find it helps if they put a note in their diary to do this. By writing it down it is like you are making an appointment with yourself, and it also acts as a reminder.

Where to look

Companies advertise jobs all over the place – from local and national papers, to recruitment agencies, their own company websites, electronic newsletters and job centres – and some don't even advertise at all. Your best bet is to keep your eye on as many of these places as possible.

In the papers

Most local papers carry some sort of appointments section, which tends to feature jobs in companies and organisations in the surrounding area. Get to know which day of the week your local paper comes out so that you can read through the jobs on offer and get your application off to the ones that you like the look of as soon as possible.

The national papers also run job advertisements for positions all over the country and beyond. Because they are larger papers with a wider readership, many of them – such as *The Guardian*, for example – advertise certain types of jobs on certain days of the week, so work out which sector's jobs appear on which days and buy the paper then, or ask your newsagent to deliver it to your house so you don't miss out.

Again, it pays to get your application in as soon as possible because hundreds of other people could be applying for the same job, and some companies get so many applications that they stop reading them after the 100th or so because they simply have too many to deal with.

Recruitment agencies

Many companies still use recruitment agencies to advertise their jobs for them and select suitable candidates for interview. Signing up with recruitment agencies can be a good idea because they do the job searching for you.

In a nutshell, the process works something like this: you send the recruitment agency your CV, or take it in yourself so you can tell them a bit about yourself and the kind of work you are looking for. When they have a job they think would suit your skills and experience, they will put you forward for it. If the company likes the sound of you, they will invite you for interview. If you don't get the job then the recruitment agency will also usually give you feedback about why your application was unsuccessful, which can be very useful.

The important thing to remember is that you should never be asked to pay for this kind of service. The recruitment agency makes their money by being paid by the company advertising the job, when they find a candidate who fits the bill. If you are ever asked to pay then refuse immediately and have nothing more to do with the organisation, as it is probably a scam.

The power of the Internet

So much of the day-to-day business of our modern world takes place over the Internet these days, and searching for jobs is no exception.

Using the Internet is a fast and efficient way of finding job vacancies and applying for them. However, once again you have to be quick off the mark because so many more people have access to the Internet that companies can receive hundreds of applications for each position they advertise online.

If you want to use the Internet to find jobs that appeal to you, there are many places to look.

'Using the Internet is a fast and efficient way of finding job vacancies and applying for them, but you have to be quick off the mark.'

There are plenty of online job sites advertising hundreds of new positions every day. Search on Google for 'job sites' and you will find them. If you decide to register your details and upload your CV to these job sites, they will email you when suitable jobs come up that match your skills and requirements. Again, as with recruitment agencies, they do the searching for you and, on the whole, you should never be asked to pay.

Many companies and organisations also advertise their job vacancies on their own websites, so if there is somewhere in particular that you would like to work, have a look at their website to see if they have a job section, and keep checking back regularly to see new jobs as they are listed. They may also offer you the option of signing up to email alerts so you will receive an email whenever they post a new job online.

Social and professional networking websites such as Facebook, Twitter and LinkedIn are also good places to look for jobs. By registering with these websites you can link up with friends, colleagues and even strangers. This in turn means you can contact present or past employees of different companies and ask them for information about jobs on offer, as well as about the pros and cons of working for their particular organisation.

Jobcentre Plus

The job centre – or labour exchange, as it was first known when it started in the early 20th century – was traditionally one of the main places where people would go to look for work.

Today, Jobcentre Plus – both online and in bricks-and-mortar premises – is part of the government's Department for Work and Pensions (DWP). It organises a variety of financial payments, or 'benefits', for people who are out of work, with the ultimate aim of helping people get off benefits and find a job.

To find your local Jobcentre Plus, go to the website (see help list) and click on 'Contact Jobcentre Plus' for more details, or look in your local phone book. You can either visit the premises in person to talk to an adviser about looking for work, or visit the Jobcentre Plus website mentioned above and search online for jobs.

Free Jobcentre Plus app

If you have an iPhone, an iPod touch or a Google Android phone then you can download the free Jobcentre Plus app, which could help you find a job in your area. You can select key locations where you're looking for work and see exactly where the vacancies are on Google maps.

The app can be used by jobseekers in England, Wales and Scotland. It searches for jobs on the Jobcentre Plus job search site, which lists over 10,000 new vacancies every working day.

You can download the app for free from iTunes.

Contact companies directly

If you can't find the job you're looking for through any of the channels mentioned above, directly contacting companies you want to work for is another approach you can take. Lots of companies are impressed by people who take the initiative, but you have to do it properly.

Firstly, try to find out the name of the right person to get in touch with. There is no point contacting the chief executive because – unless it's a tiny company with only a handful of staff – they won't be the person you need to talk to and will almost certainly be too busy to address your query. Instead, start by calling the main switchboard or contact number (find it in the phone book or by Googling the company name) and ask for the name and contact details of the person who deals with recruitment.

Next, either write them a letter or send an email explaining why you would like to work for the company, and what kind of role you are looking for. If you don't hear back from them after a couple of weeks, follow your letter up with a phone call and ask to speak to them in person to see if they have had a chance to read your initial letter, and ask them whether there might be any jobs coming up that you could apply for.

Usually, they will tell you that they will keep your details on file and let you know if anything suitable comes up, but if you really have your heart set on working for them then it's worth contacting them again from time to time (every couple of months or so) to reinforce the fact that you are serious about working there.

The advantage of this method of job hunting is that you will, hopefully, build a relationship with the person or people who look after the hiring side of things within the organisation, and may well hear about positions that are coming up before they are even advertised. However, the key with this approach is to be proactive – but avoid becoming a nuisance at all costs. You want them to think of you as tactful and polite, rather than as some kind of job stalker.

Look further afield

If all else fails and you simply have no luck finding the kind of job you are after, it could be time to consider working further afield – perhaps in another part of the country, or even overseas.

Moving away from an area you know might seem like a huge change to make, but sometimes it is the best way to find a job and get a foot on the career ladder of your choice. Don't discount it without giving it some thought.

Work for free

If you have some time on your hands, or if you feel that you are really getting nowhere when it comes to getting the kind of work you want, then it could be time to take a different tack. By offering to work for free for companies operating in the field you want to work in, you can make valuable contacts, gain experience and see if it really is the kind of job you want to do.

Volunteering

Lots of organisations use volunteers in some parts of their business. Many wouldn't be able to function without them, such as charities, hospitals, animal welfare organisations, free community newspapers, drama groups and so on.

It is very likely that there will be a charity or other non-profit organisation that does some kind of work in the area that you would like to get into, and they would almost certainly be very glad of your help. By volunteering to help out, even for only a few hours a month, you will learn a lot, add to your skills and meet people who do the kind of work you want to do. You might only be sealing envelopes in an office or running errands for a particular department, but you will get an insider's view of how things work and what goes on.

Research by the Chartered Management Institute and VSO (Voluntary Service Overseas) found that people who volunteer internationally develop expertise that addresses UK skills gaps. Out of 100 former VSO volunteers questioned, 80% believed they returned with expertise that they would not have gained in the UK. Almost all (92%) said they were now more capable of handling different cultures and 74% suggested they became better communicators. Around half also claimed that voluntary work had developed their problem solving abilities (57%) and influencing skills (46%).

Whether we like it or not, there is a lot of truth in the saying that it's not always what you know, but who you know. Giving up your time for free to help other people and increase your own experience will impress both the people you are working with, and those to whom you are applying for a job. In short, everyone wins.

'By volunteering to help out, even for only a few hours a month, you will learn a lot, add to your skills and meet people who do the kind of work you want to do.'

Work experience and internships

Another way to gain unpaid experience is by organising work experience – also often called 'internships' – with companies doing the sort of work you want to get involved in. Unlike volunteering – which can be a permanent or long-term commitment – work experience tends to be for only a short period of time; perhaps a couple of weeks or so, or a few months for internships.

It is usually done by school or university leavers – but that is not to say you shouldn't put yourself forward for these positions if you are not in this category – and is a great way to try out an industry and see if it's right for you. Of course, you won't get to do any of the big, exciting and glamorous parts of the job – you'll probably be making tea and doing lots of photocopying – but you will make good contacts, experience the industry from the inside and, if you do a good job, have an excellent chance to impress the people who make the hiring decisions. Just be prepared to be flexible and leave your ego at home.

Summing Up

- Think hard about what you really want to do, but be realistic.

- List the skills you have, and find out where there are gaps in your knowledge.

- Try to have a clear idea of who you want to work for, and why.

- Plan your job hunting strategy.

- Make the most of job hunting resources – the press, the web, agencies and Jobcentre Plus.

- Don't be afraid to contact companies directly, even if they are not advertising vacancies.

- Consider moving away to find the job that's right for you.

- Volunteering and internships give you valuable experience and contacts.

Chapter Two

Preparing Your CV

Your curriculum vitae – or CV – sums up your work, education and training experience, as well as giving your contact details and telling employers a little about what else you like to do outside of work.

In many cases, it is the first or only thing that a prospective employer will look at in order to decide if you could be the right person for the job they are looking to fill, and whether or not they should invite you for an interview.

Because of this, it pays to make sure you include every detail of your educational and employment experiences and achievements – as well as any other useful information about yourself which will make you look like the perfect candidate for the job – and really try to show your skills and knowledge in the best possible light.

What to include

Different people have varying views about exactly how the ideal CV should be set out. For example, some think CVs must be kept to one page while others think two pages are fine – although most recruiters don't have time to read anything longer than two pages, so keep it to two at the most.

One thing that is agreed on is that your CV must be clear and easy-to-read. Choose good quality white or cream paper and a black font (don't hand write it if at all possible), and stay away from fussy fonts (Times or Arial are fine).

There are also a few more basic building blocks that you should make sure you always include when putting together your CV.

'In many cases, your CV is the first or only thing a prospective employer will look at to decide if you are the right person for the job.'

Your contact details

At the top of the page put your name, address, telephone number and email address if you have one.

If you have your own professional website or a blog that clearly demonstrates more about what you do then add that too if you like, but don't put a link to anything non-professional – such as a MySpace or Facebook page – because this isn't likely to tell employers anything about your suitability for the job on offer and may even hinder your application.

So, for example, it could look something like this:

Simon Smith   Telephone: 02555 975321
The House, Anytown,   Email: simon@madeup.com
Someshire NE13 6QP   Website: www.simonppsmith.com

You don't have to include your date of birth or age, nationality or marital status unless you really want to, as these have nothing to do with your ability to do a job. Although it is illegal for employers to discriminate against you because of any of these points, some may still do so (even subconsciously).

A personal statement

This is a short paragraph which sums up the qualities and experience you have which make you suitable for the role in question. You don't have to include this, but it can be a useful addition to your CV as long as you tailor it to make it specific to the job you are applying for each time.

So, for example, if you were applying for a job as a playgroup assistant and already had experience in that field, your personal statement could sum it up by saying something like: 'I have seven years' experience of working with children, hold a current first aid certificate and am also trained in baby signing.'

Your employment history

List your employment history by starting with your most recent job and working your way backwards. Put the dates you worked there, the company name and your job title, plus a short paragraph or list of bullet points which clearly state what your responsibilities and achievements were.

For example:

February 2008–to date, Mustgo & Sons accountants, archive assistant.

- Assisting the archive manager with filing and retrieving customer information.
- Maintaining the company database.
- Dealing with Freedom of Information enquiries in the first instance.

If there are some gaps in your employment history where you were not working, put in a sentence or two to explain what you were doing during that time.

For example:

July 2007–November 2007, Volunteer at local homeless shelter whilst looking for a permanent job.

Your education and training

Again, start with your most recent qualifications and work backwards, listing the date, the name of the educational establishment or training body, the name of the qualification and the grades or level you achieved.

So, for example:

March 2008   Anytown Community College, Microsoft Office and Excel course.

2004–2007   Anytown University, BA Honours history (second class).

1998–2004   Anytown School, A-Level English (A), history (B), maths (C).

Eight GCSEs including maths and English, grades A-C.

Any other information

There may well be other things you want to mention which are not covered by your education or work history, so you could add in another short paragraph entitled 'Other information', where you can sum these up.

For example, perhaps you have gained a Duke of Edinburgh's Award, have been recognised for your contribution to your community, or something similar. Perhaps you have spent some time working as a volunteer, either here or overseas, or maybe you have done a stint as an intern somewhere.

'Most people also like to add a short paragraph about their interests outside of work. This gives you a chance to tell employers other things about you which they won't be able to see from your work and education history.'

Anything like this is well worth mentioning – especially if you are fresh into the world of work from education. Everything you can add to your CV which describes your skills in as much detail as possible will help create the best impression for prospective employers and recruiters.

Your interests

Most people also like to add a short paragraph about their interests outside of work. This gives you a chance to tell employers other things about you which they won't be able to see from your work and education history.

So, for example, you should include sports you like to take part in, as well as anything else you do in your free time, from knitting to going to the cinema, walking, amateur archaeology, reading and so on.

If you use this section wisely, you can also turn it to your advantage by tailoring what you say to fit the description of the kind of person recruiters are looking for.

For example, their job spec might say they want a 'team player'. If this is the case, you should make it clear in the employment history part of your CV when and how you have worked well as part of a team, and in the 'Interests' section you can mention any team sports you take part in. However, don't lie; if you don't play football, don't say you are the captain of your local five-a-side team because you'll eventually get found out.

CURRICULUM VITAE

Simon Smith
The House, Anytown
Someshire NE13 6QP

Telephone 02555 975321
Email simon@madeup.com
Website www.simonppsmith.com

I am a self-motivated individual with strong interpersonal and communication skills. My keen eye for detail means I enjoy meticulous work, and I pride myself on proactively tackling any challenge that comes my way.

EMPLOYMENT

February 2008–to date, Mustgo & Sons accountants, archive assistant.
- Assisting the archive manager with filing and retrieving customer information.
- Maintaining the company database.
- Dealing with Freedom of Information enquiries in the first instance.

September 2007–February 2008, Adam John Bookshop, customer service assistant.
- Serving customers and dealing with general queries about books.
- Electronic shop stock maintenance.
- Day-to-day cash handling and occasional cashing up duties.

July 2007–September 2007, volunteer at a homeless shelter whilst looking for a permanent job.

EDUCATION

January 2008 Anytown Community College, Microsoft Office and Excel course.
2004–2007 Anytown University, BA Honours history (second class).
1998–2004 Anytown School, A-Level English (A), history (B), maths (C).
Eight GCSEs including maths and English, grades A-C.

OTHER INFORMATION

Whilst at school I gained my gold Duke of Edinburgh's Award, and I also help out my father who runs the local Scout group.

INTERESTS

I enjoy art and literature, and going to the cinema and theatre. At the weekends I play for my local football team, and in the summer I like to travel around the south coast and go sea swimming.

References

You may decide to name a couple of people at the bottom of your CV who are willing to give you references, although you don't have to. Alternatively, you can wait until you are asked by a prospective employer to supply the names and contact details of your referees.

Either way, choose one person who will give you a personal reference – someone who is not a family member and has known you for at least two years – and someone who will give you a professional reference – so your current boss or someone you have worked for in the past, or a college or university lecturer or school head of year if you haven't had a job before.

The most important thing is to make sure that you have checked with these people that they are happy to give you a reference before you list them on your CV as referees. No one likes to be taken by surprise and it is bad manners to simply expect people to give you a reference without asking them first.

Mentioning disabilities

The Disability Discrimination Act 1995 makes it illegal for anyone with a disability to be discriminated against when it comes to being treated fairly and like any other candidate when applying for a job.

This means you don't have to mention on your CV that you have any disability, unless of course you want to. So think carefully about whether to disclose this sort of information because, despite the law, some people may still be discriminatory – whether consciously or subconsciously – against others with disabilities.

If you are invited for an interview and, for example, you use a wheelchair or have some other disability which means that the company might need to make some reasonable adjustments in order that you can attend it, this would be the time to bring it up.

If you do decide to mention any disability you have in your CV and believe that you have subsequently not been invited to interview and therefore discriminated against simply because of that, then talk to your local Citizens Advice Bureau for more advice. We will cover more about discrimination and your rights in general in chapter 10.

Extra polish

Aside from all the necessary points mentioned above, there are also some extra tweaks you should make to your CV to give it that little bit of extra polish to make it stand out from the crowd.

▪ Keep it short. People involved in the recruitment process will probably receive many applications for each job they are advertising, and may not always have the time to read a CV in detail unless it catches their eye. By keeping your CV short, neat and clear, you are making the recruiter's life as easy as possible and giving your CV the best chance of being read by someone who has a million and one other things to do.

▪ Tailor it to the job in question. It really pays to make sure you understand the company and the job you are applying for, so you can tailor your CV to match each separate job you apply for. So, for example, if you are applying for a job as a manager and the job advertisement says they are looking for someone who can work well under their own initiative, make sure your CV clearly shows your previous managerial experience (or at least, experience of managing tasks and projects if you don't have experience of managing teams of people). Also ensure it makes it clear that you are not the kind of person who needs their hand holding at every step of the way.

▪ Match key words. The job advertisement or job specification will almost certainly contain key words such as 'confident', 'organised', 'motivated' and so on. It seems like an obvious point to make, but by making sure your CV also includes these words it should catch the eye of the person who is reading it and looking out for someone who matches their job spec.

Summing Up

- Your CV is often the first thing an employer sees, so make sure it is accurate and includes all your details and experience.

- Keep it to a maximum of two pages, printed on white or cream paper, with no fancy fonts.

- Double check that your contact details, company names and dates of employment, education and experience are correct, and also that they are true.

- Use the 'Interests' section to highlight information about yourself and your skills that might not be apparent in the rest of your CV.

- Check with your referees that they are happy to give you a reference.

- It is up to you whether you decide to mention any disabilities you may have.

- Tailor your CV for each job you apply for, making sure it clearly shows how you have the experience they are looking for, as well as matching the key words mentioned in the job specification.

Chapter Three

The Application Process

So you've found a job you want to apply for and you've whipped your CV into shape, which means you are now ready to get down to the business of putting together your application.

Depending on what the job advertisement says, the employer might want you to send them your CV along with a covering letter explaining why you are the perfect candidate for the role. Alternatively, they may ask you to fill in a specific application form which they will send you, or even complete one online.

Writing a covering letter

If it is just your CV they want to see then tailor it to match the job you are applying for (see chapter 2) and send it with a covering letter. This is a straightforward, one-page letter in which you explain why you want the job, and why your skills and experience – or enthusiasm – make you the best choice for the role.

Your covering letter needs to be short – no more than one side of a page. Covering letters that ramble on are not read because the recruiter simply won't have the time to wade through pages and pages. It is up to your CV to really show off your skills and experience.

Another important thing to do is make sure your covering letter picks out and reflects back the key words from the job advertisement in the same way as your CV should.

So, for example, if the advertisement says the job requires an organised individual with experience of dealing with customers face to face, make sure that not only your CV but also your covering letter mentions that you have these skills and how you have used them.

'Your covering letter needs to be short – no more than one side of a page. Covering letters that ramble on and on are not read because the recruiter simply won't have the time to wade through pages and pages.'

The House
Anytown
Someshire NE13 6QP

24 June 2010

Steven Mustgo
Mustgo & Sons
Office House
Winding Street
London P12 Q8S

Dear Mr Mustgo

Please find enclosed my CV, in response to the job advertisement you placed in yesterday's *Daily Gazette* for an archive manager.

I have worked as an archive assistant for the past two years and am now keen to take the next step up to become an archive manager at a larger firm, such as yours.

My current role involves filing and retrieving customer information, maintaining the company database and dealing with Freedom of Information enquiries – amongst other responsibilities. I am confident that I have the skills and experience which will take me to the next level and make me an ideal candidate for the position you are looking to fill.

I would welcome the opportunity to talk to you further about what I can offer Mustgo & Sons, and look forward to hearing from you soon.

Yours sincerely

Simon Smith

Type up and print out your covering letter, rather than writing it by hand if possible, and check for spelling errors before you print it. It also looks more professional if your CV and covering letter are printed out on the same coloured paper – preferably white or cream – using the same simple font throughout both.

Filling in application forms

Some companies – usually larger organisations – will send you an application form to fill in rather than asking you to simply send them a CV and covering letter. Because they probably expect to receive a large number of applications, this makes it easier for them to compare candidates' applications side by side and select a shortlist of those people they would like to see for interview.

One of the main methods that companies use to compile a shortlist is to pick out those candidates whose skills most closely match the ones listed in the job advertisement. However, don't be put off. By taking the time to carefully read the job spec and making sure you match your responses to the key words and skills that the employer is looking for, you will give yourself the best chance of submitting a successful application.

A good tip is to treat an application form a bit like an exam paper. Before you start to fill it in, read through the whole thing once or twice so you get a clear idea of the information you are being asked to provide. It is also a good idea to photocopy the form or print off another copy so that if you are filling it in by hand rather than on a computer, you can do a rough version first and correct any mistakes before completing the actual form.

The form will usually begin by getting you to fill in boxes with details about your address, education and work experience, and you can use the information from your CV to complete these fields.

It will then probably include some questions about why you think you are suited to the particular job on offer, and may even ask you for some examples of situations where you have demonstrated particular skills in the past. Have a look at chapter 4 for some tips about how to answer questions such as 'why are you interested in this job?', 'what qualities can you bring to this position?' and 'what are your goals for the future?'.

'By taking the time to carefully read the job spec and making sure you match your responses to the key words and skills that the employer is looking for, you will give yourself the best chance of submitting a successful application.'

Once again, make sure your answers include key words from the job advertisement or job spec, so that the employer can see that you have the qualities and experience they are looking to find in the person they will choose to fill the role in question.

Online applications

Completing online applications works in much the same way as ordinary paper application forms, but there are a few extra things to think about.

Firstly, don't rush it. Many people find that it is easier to make spelling errors when typing rather than writing by hand. This is because when you are typing you know what you think you have written, but very often this is not what you have actually written.

Again, it is a good idea to print out a copy of the application form if at all possible – or if you can't do this, write the questions and your responses on some scrap paper first – so that you can have a practice run of filling it in before you send off your final completed version. Alternatively, if you are able to download the form onto your computer, you could save your rough copy electronically.

Once you are happy with what you have written, type your responses into the online form – use your computer's spellchecker to ensure you haven't missed any mistakes – and make sure you have saved a copy, either electronically or by printing one out, before you send it off.

References

We've talked about references in detail in chapter 2, but it is worth mentioning them again here. If the application form asks you to put the names and contact details of any referees, then don't forget to check with them that they are happy to be listed before you submit your application.

Sending it off

We've already mentioned the importance of keeping a copy of your completed application form, but the other key part about submitting any application is to make sure you send it in on time.

The job advertisement or job spec you will have been sent will include a closing date by which all applications must be received. If yours arrives after this date then it will almost certainly not be considered – in fact, employers who are expecting a large number of responses to their job ads will be grateful that you have given them an easy way of filtering your application straight into the bin and saved them the hassle of reading it.

If you are posting your application then bear in mind that while first class post is supposed to take one day, and second class a couple of days, this isn't guaranteed. If you want to make sure your application gets there the next day then go in to your local Post Office and pay a little extra to send it by Special Delivery™. This guarantees that it will arrive on the following day, and requires the recipient to sign for it. If you have access to a computer, you can then track the progress of your letter online and see when it is signed for, and by whom.

If your application is not so urgent – or you haven't left it until the last minute – but you would still like to know when it's received at the other end, then consider sending it by first or second class recorded delivery post. This also requires it to be signed for at its destination, so you can track it online.

Sending it in this way, so that someone signs for it when it is received, is also helpful if you need to follow up the progress of your application. You will at least know that it has been received at the other end.

Following up

Some job adverts will specify how long you could expect to wait before hearing whether your application has been successful or not. However, many companies don't want to tie themselves down to a particular date in case the process of sifting all the applications takes them longer than they expect.

As mentioned overleaf, if you have sent off your application using a postal option that requires a signature from the receiver, you can track its progress online and you will know when it has been received. Similarly, if you have submitted your application online then you may have received an automated confirmation email that it has arrived.

If you are not sure that your application has got to where it needs to be, it is perfectly acceptable to ring the company and ask to speak to the person to whom you sent the application (if you know their name, or ask for the HR department or hiring manager if you don't) to confirm that they have it. Simply explain that you want to make sure that they have received your application, and then ask them when you might expect to hear their decision. Unless the person you are talking to is particularly chatty then leave it at that and don't badger them. They've probably got enough to do and, if it's a large company that you've applied to, they might be extremely busy dealing with hundreds of applications for more than one position at any one time.

After that, if it has been more than two weeks since you sent in your application and you know that it was received but you still haven't heard whether you've been successful so far, don't be afraid of contacting the company to find out. Most organisations will only take a couple of weeks to come up with a shortlist of candidates whom they want to see at interview. If you have been waiting to hear for longer than that, a short telephone call or email asking about the progress of your application is usually not frowned upon by employers – unless, of course, the job advertisement stated right from the start that unsuccessful candidates or those who were not shortlisted for interview would not be contacted.

Similarly, if the job advertisement or job spec gave a date by which you could expect to hear their decision, and you still haven't heard after that time, then by all means get in touch with them and chase them up. As with all contact you might have with prospective employers, keep it short and polite. You never know, your initiative could always be seen as another positive trait that might just clinch you the job.

'If you are not sure that your application has got to where it needs to be, it is perfectly acceptable to ring the company and ask to speak to the person to whom you sent the application.'

Summing Up

- Check whether you need to apply by sending your CV and a covering letter, or by filling in an application form.

- Make sure your covering letter is short, correctly spelled and printed on paper which matches your CV.

- Do a rough version of your covering letter and any application forms before you type out or fill in the actual one you are going to send off.

- As with your CV, your covering letter or application form should contain the key words from the job ad to show how your experience matches what the company is looking for.

- Always keep a copy of what you are sending.

- Send all applications off in good time.

- Use recorded or signed-for postal delivery options if you want to be sure your application gets there on time and is received by the right person.

- It is fine to ring or email to check that your application has been received.

- If you haven't heard from the company after two weeks, don't be afraid to get in touch with them to check the progress of your application.

- Always be polite, don't badger or threaten the person you speak to, and keep your conversations short and to the point.

'If you haven't heard from the company after two weeks, don't be afraid to get in touch with them to check the progress of your application.'

Chapter Four

Going for an Interview

If the company likes the sound of you from your CV, covering letter or application form, they will invite you in for an interview. What they want to find out is how well your skills and experience match the skillset – or 'core competencies' – of the position they are looking to fill.

Just as there is plenty of preparation to do when completing your initial application, there is also lots you can do to make sure your interview goes as well as possible.

Do your research

The secret to performing well in interviews is preparation and research. You will impress the interviewer(s) if you can show that you have researched the company, its ethics and culture, and the role you are applying for.

When you get invited for interview, the company may send you some information about what it does, or direct you to its website so you can find out more. This is not optional – they want you to read up on them, get to know what they do and who they do it for.

But don't just stop there. Use the Internet – at your local library if you don't have it at home – to find out even more about the company you are going to see. Type their name into a search engine – such as Google – and read the information that comes up about them. Find out if they have been in the news recently, and for what. Perhaps they've expanded, made some investment in their business, or won an award.

'Just as there is plenty of preparation to do when completing your initial application, there is also lots you can do to make sure your interview goes as well as possible.'

Another way to learn more about a company is by using social networking websites – such as Facebook, Twitter or FriendsReunited – to contact other people who work or have worked at the company, and get their take on the organisation. This can give you an insider's view, and will probably give you a good idea of the pros and cons of working there.

The interviewer also wants to hear you explain how your skills and experience match the position you are being interviewed for, so your research should also involve finding out more about the job in question. Social networking can help you here as well, but if you can't talk to someone who already works for the company doing the job you want to do, try to find someone somewhere else who is doing something similar.

The more you can find out through your own research, rather than from simply reading and digesting the information which the company itself sends you, the better you will look.

Doing your own research shows that you are proactive and willing to go the extra mile. Be sure that you make it clear in the interview that you have done so by telling them what you've found out, such as 'I saw on the BBC news website that your chief executive has just been awarded an OBE,' or 'I read the story in the local paper about you taking on 20 new staff last month.'

Who are you going to meet?

When you are invited to attend an interview, you will be told when and where it will be held, and possibly the names and job titles of the person or people who are going to be interviewing you.

Job interviews can be conducted by one or more people. You might be interviewed by someone from the Human Resources (HR) department, by the person who would be your boss or line manager, or even their boss, or perhaps a panel made up of some or all of these people, and others.

If your invitation to interview doesn't mention who these people will be, it is worth calling the HR department or asking the person who contacted you who you will be interviewed by. By finding out whether you will be meeting your

'The interviewer also wants to hear you explain how your skills and experience match the position you are interviewing for, so your research should also involve finding out more about the job in question.'

prospective boss, a recruitment manager or someone else from the company, you can tailor your preparation so that you can ask, and are ready to answer, the sorts of questions that these different people may have.

For example, if you are meeting the person who would be your boss, they might want to find out how you are going to fit into the mix of staff they already have, so they could ask you questions about teamwork, how you deal with different people, whether you consider yourself to be co-operative, how you cope under pressure and so on.

If you are being interviewed by someone from HR, they are likely to ask you questions about your salary expectations, what sort of training you've had and how long the notice period for your current job is (if you have one).

Questions you will probably be asked – and things not to say

If you have got as far as the interview stage, it means that the company likes the sound of you from your CV and covering letter. However, now they want to meet you and find out more about you.

They will almost certainly be interviewing more than one person for the same position, and one of the ways they use to decide who is most suited for the job is to ask each candidate a pretty standard set of questions.

Below are some of the most common questions that you can expect to be asked at a job interview. Work out what you would say in response to each of these, making sure your answers refer to the skills you have developed through the jobs or training you have done so far. You could even try role-playing these with a friend to get some practice.

How would you describe yourself?

It is fine to say you are 'friendly' or 'organised' or other positive things, but what they are really looking for are attributes that explain why you are the right person for the position they are looking to fill.

Don't say: 'I'm terrible at getting up in the mornings and I'm always late.'

Do say: 'I love to try new things and am able to think clearly under pressure.'

Why are you interested in this job?

Your answer should be about wanting to increase your responsibilities, trying a new challenge and expanding your knowledge.

Don't say: 'I heard you have a much better canteen than where I work now.'

Do say: 'I know that your company is very proactive about staff training and I'm always keen to add to my skills.'

What do you think the job entails?

If you are applying for the job then you've probably done something similar before, or you think that your skills will fit what they are looking for. If not, make sure you do your research before the interview to find out more about the position in question.

Don't say: 'I don't really know, but I hate where I work now and want a change.'

Do say: 'I had quite a good idea, but then I spoke to someone I know who works here and they have explained a bit more about it to me' (and then talk about what you've found out about the job).

What qualities do you think you can bring to this position?

You have applied for this job because you know, or think, you can do it. As well as that, you should have made yourself familiar with the job spec they sent out so you know what kind of person they are looking for. Your answer to this question needs to match the skills you already have with the skills they are looking for.

Don't say: 'I'm a bit of a joker and every office needs one of those.'

Do say: 'I have lots of transferable skills which match what you're looking for' (and then describe them).

What are your strengths?

Talk about things you have achieved which are relevant to the job you are applying for, and mention positive qualities about yourself such as being motivated, organised or confident. For example, if the job is all about organisation and deadlines, give examples which demonstrate how you have used your skills in these areas.

Don't say: 'My boss says I can talk for England.'

Do say: 'I consider myself to be very flexible and work hard to always see other points of view' (and then give examples).

What are your weaknesses?

This is almost a trick question so be careful not to put your foot in it here by reeling out a list of things you don't think you are good at. For example, don't say things like 'I hate talking on the phone'. Instead, mention weaknesses which could also be considered plus points, such as 'I'm a bit of a perfectionist'.

Don't say: 'I'm not really a people person.'

Do say: 'I can never leave a job unfinished.'

What has been the biggest challenge you've ever faced in your career?

Again, keep it work-related and talk about a challenge you've met and overcome, but be sure to emphasise the positive rather than making it sound negative.

Don't say: 'I didn't like my colleague so I made his life a misery until he had enough and left.'

Do say: 'I was passed over for promotion so studied for some extra qualifications in the evening to boost my skills.'

Why do you want to leave your current job?

Never say anything bad about your last employer, even if you hated everything about working there. The reasons you give for wanting to leave should always be to do with looking for more responsibility, training opportunities or an increase in salary.

Don't say: 'They think I am stealing and so I want to leave before they sack me.'

Do say: 'It is a small company with limited opportunities to progress, so I would like to further my career somewhere that has a bit more to offer.'

What do you know about our company?

This is your chance to impress by showing you have done your research. A great way to prove that you want to work somewhere is by demonstrating that you are interested in the company and what they do. If they've expanded, won an award or a new contract recently, mention that you've heard about it.

Don't say: 'You have a good pension scheme and lots of my mates work here.'

Do say: 'My research shows that you have an excellent reputation for being a forward-looking and proactive company, which is probably why you won that award for innovation last year.'

'Never say anything bad about your last employer, even if you hated everything about working there.'

40

How would your colleagues describe you?

Now is your chance to say nice things about yourself without appearing big-headed. Choose things like 'I'm friendly, polite, kind, organised' and so on, but don't mention anything that's not true in case you get caught out at a later stage.

Don't say: 'As the first one on stage at the Christmas party karaoke.'

Do say: 'I'm the first one to volunteer to stay late and finish the job in hand.'

What are your goals for the future?

Again, these should be to do with the job. Don't say anything negative, such as 'I don't really want to work but I've got bills to pay'. Instead, say things like 'I am keen to continue to build on my strong communication skills and believe your company is the ideal place to do this'.

Don't say: 'To win the lottery and retire at 35.'

Do say: 'To build an interesting and productive career, and leave a lasting good impression wherever I work.'

What salary are you looking for?

Try to do everything you can not to answer this question, because if you say a figure which is lower than what they had in mind then they will be very pleased and offer you that. On the other hand, if you say a figure which is way too high then you might just be edging yourself out of the running. It is best to try to leave salary talk for the second interview, or for when you have been offered the job, as you will have a bit more leverage for negotiation because you already know they want you in the role.

Don't say: 'I am clearly worth £100,000 a year, so if you can't match that then I'm off.'

Do say: 'Tell me what you had in mind first, and then I will tell you if that is around the figure that I am looking for.'

Questions you don't have to answer

Prospective employers are forbidden by law from discriminating against job hunters during the recruitment process. People should be chosen for employment solely on the skills they have which will enable them to do the job.

This means that there are certain questions employers are not allowed to ask you, and if they do you can refuse to answer them. These include questions about your sexual orientation, religious beliefs or plans to have children (including – if you are a woman – whether you are currently pregnant or not).

You should also be on the look out for interviewers who try to ask about these things in a roundabout way. So, for example, they might say 'And what does your husband think about you applying for this job?' or 'We make a big deal about Christmas in this office, so I hope that's not going to be a problem for you?'

'Prospective employers are forbidden by law from discriminating against job hunters during the recruitment process.'

On the other hand, there are some personal questions that employers are allowed to ask in relation to the specific position they are trying to fill. For example, the Disability Discrimination Act allows an employer to ask whether you have any disability – such as mobility issues which may require you to use a wheelchair – so that they can hold the interview in a suitable room that you can easily access and make sure that whatever disabilities you may have would not affect your ability to do the job, after a reasonable adjustment, if necessary.

Most employers abide by the law and are sensible about these issues, but it pays to know your rights. In fact, if you believe that you have been discriminated against, you might be able to take the company to an employment tribunal (see chapter 10 for more details).

Questions you should ask

So you've done your research and you know what your answers are going to be to some of the most common questions the interviewer might ask, but what do you want ask them?

Have they covered everything you wanted to know about the job in question? Do you know when you could expect to hear from them about whether you have got the job or not? Are you clear about exactly what the job entails? If they were to offer you the job, do you think you have enough information to decide whether you want to accept it?

Asking questions yourself shows that you are engaged in the recruitment process and interested in the position you are applying for. It also helps you have more of a conversation with the interviewer, rather than just sitting there and fielding their questions. Many interviewers will judge you as much on the questions you ask them as they do on the answers you give to their questions.

Good examples of questions to ask include:

- What's the most important thing I could do in my first three months of working here?

- What are the dynamics of the team I would be joining?

- Is there a probation period for this job?

- What sort of career progression could I expect from this role?

- Why did the last person leave this job, and where did they go?

- Can you tell me more about the line-management structure for this position?

- When might I expect to hear whether my application has been successful?

If the job advertisement or your initial contact with company has not made it clear what the salary is for the job, you might be tempted to ask at your first interview. Opinions about this differ, but on the whole it is considered good manners not to mention money at your first meeting. If you are invited for a second interview then you can ask at the end of that, if they still haven't volunteered the information. Alternatively, you could ask when they let you know that they want to offer you the job. For tips about salary negotiation, see chapter 5.

'Asking questions yourself shows that you are engaged in the recruitment process and interested in the position you are applying for.'

Assessment centres

Some companies use assessment centres as a form of interview. They are a way for them to meet, assess and interview a number of people all at the same time, and are most often used when there is more than one job to be filled.

Assessment centres usually involve all prospective candidates for a job going to the company at the same time for a day, or part of a day, where you will meet other staff and be set a series of group and individual tasks in order to determine what sort of personality you are and if you are suitable for the job in question.

If you are invited to attend an assessment centre as part of your interview process then be prepared to take part in role-play exercises. These help your prospective employer judge things like whether you are a team player, if you can think creatively and make fast, accurate judgements, as well as whether you have leadership potential or are the kind of person who prefers to work in the background.

You might also be expected to give a presentation of some sort. This could be on a topic given to you on the day, or you might be told before you come to the assessment what the topic is so you can prepare what you are going to say in advance. The topic could be something generic which they ask everybody, such as talking about your hobbies or why you enjoyed a particular holiday, or it could be something specific to the job for which you are applying, such as analysing sales figures or talking about one of the company's products.

The downside to assessment centres is that they can be a long and tiring day, and an intense experience. You have to be on the ball all the time and do your best to outshine the competition.

However, if you prepare in advance and make sure you know your stuff, assessment centres can be a great experience because you will get to meet lots of people, see where you might end up working and get a feel for the atmosphere of the company. They also give you a chance to promote yourself directly to the people who will be deciding who they want to hire.

The second interview

You might be invited to attend a second interview, which can be very different from the first one. Sometimes the first interview is more formal and the second one less so, or vice versa.

The reason for a second interview might be that other staff members want to meet you. It could be that the first interview is what is known as a 'sift' – where the company sees lots of people for short interviews in quick succession to help them narrow down a smaller number of candidates they want to see again. The second might be so that the person in authority, such as the head of the department in which you are going to be working, can meet you and be able to say that they have interviewed you.

How to dress

Some companies – such as those in the creative industries like design and media – have a more relaxed attitude towards what their staff wear to work than other organisations such as law firms or accountancy practices.

However, wherever you are applying for a job, the general rule is that it pays to look smart for your interview. As the saying goes, you never get a second chance to make a first impression, so make sure that the way you look portrays you in the best light possible.

Some people like to buy a new outfit to make themselves feel special or more confident, while others prefer to wear the lucky shoes which they've worn for every job interview they've ever had. It's not compulsory to wear a suit but whatever you choose to wear should be neat, clean and in good condition. Shoes should be polished, shirts should be ironed and anything with rips, holes, stains or smells should be left in your wardrobe.

Don't wear anything too small, too tight or too short – you don't want to look uncomfortable or dressed for the wrong occasion. Similarly, don't go for unseasonal outfits – no summer dresses or sandals in winter, and no shorts at any time of year (unless your interview is to be a lifeguard!).

'It's not compulsory to wear a suit but whatever you choose to wear should be neat, clean and in good condition.'

You're not going clubbing, to the beach or to the pub; you're going for a job interview, so keep it neat and modest. Cover up any tattoos and unusual body piercings if you have them, avoid strong perfume or aftershave, keep make-up to a minimum and have clean and tidy hair.

If you can't bear to leave the house without somehow expressing a bit of your personality through what you wear, try to confine it to your accessories rather than your entire look. Crazy cufflinks or a statement bag will be enough.

And finally, get your outfit ready the night before so that you can make sure it is clean and in a good state. This will save you from rushing about in the morning deciding what to wear.

Body language and manners

'When you meet your interviewer(s), make sure you smile, say hello and shake their hand with a firm – but not bone-crunching – grip.'

Some experts believe that as much as 93% of our communication is through non-verbal signals – or body language. Certainly, making a good impression when you first meet someone is as much to do with what you don't say, as what you do.

When you meet your interviewer(s), make sure you smile, say hello and shake their hand with a firm – but not bone-crunching – grip. Try to maintain eye contact with whomever is talking to you rather than looking at the ground, your hands or around the room, as this will make you appear more confident. Don't slouch in your seat or you will look bored, and stifle any yawns for the same reason.

Try not to cross your arms or legs, because this creates a subconscious barrier between you and the interviewer, and even if they don't know the rules of body language they will pick up on this. Crossing arms and legs can also make you more tense. You will feel much more relaxed if you sit up straight with both feet on the floor and your hands either resting in your lap or on the table in front of you, if there is one.

Maintaining good manners is also important and shows the interviewer that you respect them and the time they are giving up to see you. Don't chew gum, pick your fingers (or anything else) or play with your hair, no matter how nervous you are. And make sure you turn off your mobile phone. If you forget and it rings, apologise and turn it off immediately.

Don't be late – and plan your route to the interview

Being late is disrespectful and, unless you have a really good excuse, will put you in the interviewer's bad books straightaway. Remember, they probably have other candidates to see, so if you are late you could be holding all those people up as well. In extreme cases, you might forfeit your interview if you are late, and miss the chance of getting the job you wanted.

If you are on your way to the interview and realise you are going to be late, call the company as soon as you can to apologise and let them know when you expect to arrive.

One way to make sure you won't be late is to plan your route to the interview in advance. The chances are that you might never have been to the company's offices or premises before, so doing a 'dry run' beforehand – whether that's driving yourself there, catching the bus or train, or however you are going to get to the interview – means that you will have a chance to get to know the route and work out how long it will take you on the day. Remember to factor in extra time if you will be travelling in the rush hour on the day of your interview.

Planning it out beforehand means it's also one less thing to worry about on the day. At least you will know where you are going, how to get there and how long it should take you. And make sure you take the company's switchboard or general phone number with you so that you can call in if you end up running late.

Dealing with nerves and keeping calm

Almost everyone gets nervous before a job interview, especially if you have to do a presentation, but it's important not to let your nerves show too much or get in the way of your performance.

If you have done your preparation and research properly, know who you are going to see and how to get to where you are going then you should be pretty well-equipped to deal with the interview.

Try to get an early night the night before, and eat some breakfast in the morning. Have a hanky with you for runny nose, sweaty palm or make-up smudge emergencies, and don't forget to breathe.

'Try to get an early night the night before, and eat some breakfast in the morning. Have a hanky with you for runny nose, sweaty palm or make-up smudge emergencies, and don't forget to breathe.'

Before you go in to the interview, sit quietly and take four or five slow, deep breaths in through your nose and out through your mouth to calm you down a little. Keep a small bottle of water with you so you can take a few sips if you need to ward off a dry mouth, which lots of people suffer from when they have to speak in unfamiliar situations.

Once you are in the interview, remember the body language techniques mentioned earlier, and don't be afraid to take your time answering the questions. If you don't understand something someone has said, or you didn't hear properly, ask them to repeat or rephrase their question.

Remember: it's not a criminal interrogation, it's just a job interview. Its purpose is just as much for you to find out whether you like the company as it is for the company to see if it likes you.

Practice interviews

If you haven't had any or many job interviews in the past, or it's been a while since your last one and you think you are going to get really nervous and make a mess of it, ask a friend or family member to run through a few practice interviews with you before the real thing.

Go through the 'questions you will probably be asked' so that you feel confident that you have got the answers lodged in your memory.

Aside from those, it doesn't really matter what other questions your practice interview contains. In fact, the stranger, ruder or tougher, the better. The point of this exercise is to get you thinking on your feet, practising good body language, eye-contact and breathing techniques, and to be able to calmly and politely answer anything that is thrown at you.

After all, practice makes perfect, so the more you do, the more used to the interview process you will become.

Summing Up

- Good research is the key to doing well at an interview.
- Find out who you are going to meet, when and where.
- Prepare yourself for the inevitable questions and know how you will answer them.
- Know what questions you don't have to answer.
- Work out some really good questions you want to ask them.
- Try to avoid talking about salary at a first interview.
- Understand what's different about second interviews and assessment centres.
- Present yourself well, be on time and learn how to keep calm.
- If you're feeling a little rusty, get some interview practice in.

Chapter Five

How to Deal with a Job Offer

You've done your research, applied for the job, been for the interview and obviously done well because you've had a phone call and all the hard work has paid off because they've offered you the job.

Yes, the hard part is over, but you've still got a little more work to do before you start.

Get it in writing

Firstly, ask the company to send you the offer in writing, along with any other paperwork, including your contract, so that you can have a good look at what they expect from you and what they are offering in terms of salary, holiday and other benefits.

Ask for time to consider

You don't have to rush into accepting the job, although you don't want to hang about too long. Ask for at least 24 hours to make your decision so that you can read the contract and all other paperwork properly and talk to your friends and family if you need to, ensuring you are making the right choice.

'You don't have to rush into accepting the job, although you don't want to hang about too long.'

If the company offering you the job is trying to push you to accept their offer the minute they have made it, stand your ground and insist on at least having the evening to think about it, and make sure you have all the paperwork at hand. If they really want you for the job, rather than just wanting any old person to fill the position, then they will wait.

Similarly, if you have gone through a recruitment agency to find a job, they will be the one to tell you about the job offer that is being made to you, and you can make the same demands of them. Ask for time to consider and to be sent the relevant paperwork. Don't let them hurry you for an on-the-spot decision. Yes, they want to do a good job for their client (the company) which is paying them to find someone for the role, but it is in your interest as well as theirs for you to be sure you want to accept it. No company wants someone to start and then leave after a few weeks because they didn't really want the job in the first place.

Salary and other negotiations

The company might have been clear from the start about the salary by putting it in the job advertisement. If not, the subject of salary may well have come up in your interview, but if it didn't or if you are not quite happy with the level of the salary they are offering, now is the time to negotiate.

To find out what the going rate for the job you've been offered is, do some research into what similar companies are paying for similar jobs. This is called the 'market rate' for the job, and it will help you work out what you should be paid, although it is worth remembering that smaller companies will probably pay a little less than larger ones.

The next step is the one that takes nerves of steel. Ask for a little more than the market rate. This is because you will have room to negotiate downwards, so that the company feels it has done a deal with you and got your services for a good price.

For example, your research might show that people doing similar jobs for similar companies get paid around £15,500 per year for what they do. If your job offer comes with a salary of £14,000, go back to the company and say that you have done some research into the market rate for that particular position and that you were hoping to be paid something in the region of £16,500.

They may come back and say they won't negotiate at all, they may offer you the £16,500 that you asked for, or they may up their offer a bit but not quite reach what you had in mind.

The important thing to remember is don't panic and don't get stroppy. If their offer is almost there, you could accept it but ask for your next salary review (which most companies hold annually) to be brought forward to six months rather than a year later. This is also the time to promise that you will do an excellent job for them and you are sure that within the first six months they will clearly be able to see why you are worth a little more.

Also, take a careful look at the whole package they are offering – not just the salary. A job is not just about money. If the salary is not quite what you would have hoped for then there are other things to take into consideration. For example, perhaps you get more than the statutory 28 days holiday for full-time workers. Maybe the company still offers a final salary pension (very rare these days, but a good benefit). Perhaps they are the leader in their field and you have always dreamed of working for them.

If you still feel that the salary offer and total package is too low, and the company won't budge on negotiations, you have to decide whether you really want, and can afford, to accept the position.

'Take a careful look at the whole package they are offering – not just the salary. A job is not just about money.'

References

When you apply for a job, most companies will ask you to provide the names and contact details of at least two referees that they can contact to verify that you are who you say you are and that you are of 'good character'.

They will usually ask you to name someone who will give you a professional reference – usually your current or most recent employer, if you have one – and a personal reference, from someone you have known for at least two years who is not a family member.

The company will then write to these people to ask them a little bit about you and how they know you, as well as how well they think you could do the job you have applied for. This allows the company to confirm your identity and get another point of view about your suitability for the position.

Because you might not want your current employer to know that you are looking for a new job, you can ask that the company you are interviewing with does not take up your professional reference until after they have made you a formal offer of a job. However, this could mean that if and when they do offer you the job, it is conditional on them getting a satisfactory response from your referees.

It is not illegal for your present or previous employer to give you a bad reference but it has to be fair, accurate and true, so they have to be very careful how they phrase their response. They can, however, refuse to give you a reference, which looks just as bad as if they said terrible things about you.

While it is highly unlikely that your prospective new employer would withdraw their job offer to you in light of something one of your referees had said, it could happen if the referees' responses showed that you had lied about your past experience or your identity. However, if you have accepted their offer and they then withdraw it, you might be able to claim compensation for breach of contract. If you have a dispute you can contact a solicitor or the Citizens Advice Bureau for further advice.

Medicals

Some companies also have a policy of requiring applicants to undergo a medical – or at least make their medical history available to the employer – before their contract is finalised. Again, if you don't meet their requirements then your offer could be withdrawn, or no offer made.

The legalities

There are certain legalities that you need to watch out for when reading through your new contract.

Pay

You can expect to be paid at least the national minimum hourly wage which, at the time of going to press, in the UK is:

- £5.80 for workers aged 22 and over.
- £4.83 for workers aged 18-21.
- £3.57 for workers aged 16-17 (above school leaving age but under 18).

For more details about the national minimum wage in the UK, go to www.direct.gov.uk and search for 'minimum wage'.

Probationary period

Most companies expect new staff to complete a probationary period of anything up to six months, so that both parties can see that they are suited to the job. During this time you should expect to receive all necessary training in order to do your job to a reasonable level, and you will probably have regular meetings with your boss or line manager to discuss and measure your progress.

Another important point about being on probation is that the company can get rid of you with a much shorter notice period, but you can usually also give them shorter notice if you wish to leave within this time. They can also extend your probation if you reach the end of it and they are still not quite happy with your progress.

However, all of this must be included in your contract, which must state how long your probation will be, what your notice period is during your probation – both the notice that the company has to give if they want you to leave, as well as how long you must give them if you want to go – and the fact that they can extend your probation if they wish.

'Most companies expect new staff to complete a probationary period of anything up to six months, so that both parties can see that they are suited to the job.'

Annual leave

All full-time workers in the UK are entitled to at least 5.6 weeks' paid holiday – also called annual leave – every year, which can include bank and public holidays if your employer so wishes. Part-time staff are entitled to the same amount pro rata so, for example, if you work only three days a week you will get 5.6 times your usual working week, which works out at 16.8 days' leave per year.

This is the minimum that the law requires, but some employers give their staff more than this, and some companies let you build up more holiday days the longer you have worked for them.

However, your employer is allowed to decide when you can take your holiday time, and whether they include bank holidays in your leave entitlement. For example, if you work in a shop then your employer might not want staff taking time off over the Christmas period as that is a busy time for them. Similarly, some factories have set 'shut-down periods' for a couple of weeks in the summer and over Christmas, and you may have to take your holiday then, when production effectively stops.

Any conditions relating to your annual leave will be made clear in your contract, so read it carefully before you accept a new job to make sure you understand any restrictions your employer wants to impose.

Other points to remember:

'The law states that you're entitled to take your annual leave from the time you begin your job, although it's not advisable to start a new role and then immediately ask for two weeks off.'

- The law states that you're entitled to take your annual leave from the time you begin your job, although it's not advisable to start a new role and then immediately ask for two weeks off.

- You will get paid your normal pay rate for any days you take as holiday.

- When you leave a job, you are entitled to be paid for any annual leave that you haven't taken.

- You are entitled to take your holiday leave throughout ordinary and additional maternity leave and paternity and adoption leave.

- You don't have an automatic right to paid leave on bank and public holidays, although many people receive the day off work. Any right to time off or extra pay for working on a bank holiday depends on the terms of your contract of employment. There are eight permanent bank and public holidays in England and Wales, nine in Scotland and 10 in Northern Ireland.

Sick pay

You are entitled to sick pay if you have to take time off work due to illness, and your contract must have all the details in it.

There are two types of sick pay:

- Company sick pay (also called contractual or occupational sick pay).
- Statutory Sick Pay (SSP).

Company sick pay

Your employer may well run their own company sick pay scheme, the details of which will be in your contract. If they don't run their own scheme then it must say so in your contract, and they have to pay you Statutory Sick Pay if you are eligible. Company sick pay cannot pay you less than you are entitled to through Statutory Sick Pay.

Your entitlement to company sick pay usually starts once you have completed your probationary period. It means you should receive your normal pay while you are off work due to illness for a number of weeks specified by your employer, and then half pay for a further number of weeks of their choosing, after which any more sick leave will be unpaid. Again, your contract will state how long this period is for.

Proof of sickness

Your employer will probably have a set procedure that they wish you to follow when you are sick – for example, calling your line manager first thing in the morning to let them know you are going to be off, and to tell them when you expect to be back at work.

Most employers let you 'self-certify' – in other words, declare yourself sick – for any period up to one week. However, they will usually expect you to produce a doctor's certificate after you have been off for seven days – now called a 'fit note' – which will tell your employer when they can expect you back at work, and whether they need to make any adjustments to your working conditions on your return.

Statutory Sick Pay

Statutory Sick Pay (SSP) is paid by your employer for up to 28 weeks. At the time of going to press, you are entitled to SSP at a standard rate of £79.15 a week, even if you've only just started working for a company, if:

- You're sick for at least four days in a row (including weekends, bank holidays and days that you do not normally work).
- You're earning at least £95 a week.

In order to get SSP, you must tell your employer that you are sick and, if they ask you to, provide a medical certificate from the eighth day of your illness.

Bonuses

Some companies reward their staff by paying them an extra bonus at a certain point in the year.

If you find that the bonus is part of your salary package, your contract must state that you will get a certain amount as a set salary with a variable bonus on top.

However, these bonuses often depend on certain conditions or targets being met during the year – either by you as an individual or by the performance of the company as a whole – and so are not guaranteed. Read the conditions carefully, and be aware that this extra bonus money is not a definite extra that you are entitled to.

Make sure you are happy before you sign

It pays to think very carefully about the salary and other benefits package which the company is offering you for the role, so make sure that you are happy to sign a contract and agree to their terms and conditions before you start the job.

Once you begin working for them, it becomes much harder to renegotiate something that you have already agreed to, and it certainly won't put you in their good books.

How to accept an offer

Once you've read through all the paperwork and your contract, spoken to the company's HR department or the person who is hiring you in order to iron out any queries you might have, and you are happy with the job offer and its conditions, it's time to formally accept.

While a verbal acceptance is binding, it is best to put it in writing – and keep a copy for yourself – so that everyone involved has a record.

Emails are probably acceptable these days, but a clear, straightforward letter on plain paper (unlined if possible – you don't want it to look like you've torn it out of an exercise book!) is still the best, most professional way to send your acceptance. You will also need to sign your contract and include that with your acceptance letter. The company should send you two copies of your contract to sign – one to send back to them and one to keep yourself.

Address your acceptance to the person who sent you your offer letter, and ask them to confirm that they have received your letter so that you know it got to them. If you want to make extra sure, you can send it using recorded delivery post at the Post Office, which means someone will have to sign for it at the other end and you can track the progress of your letter.

'It pays to think very carefully about the salary and other benefits package which the company is offering you for the role, so make sure that you are happy to sign a contract and agree to their terms and conditions before you start the job.'

How to reject an offer

If you decide to decline a job offer, putting it in writing is also the best way.

You can keep it short and sweet, and you don't have to go into long-winded detail about why you are turning their offer down. Be polite and simply thank them for their offer, say you very much enjoyed meeting them and that you would be delighted if, one day in the future, it turned out that your career path brought you back in touch with them again.

Even if the reason you are rejecting their offer is because you couldn't come to an agreement about some point in the contract, you thought the salary was stingy, or you decided you didn't like the person who interviewed you and thought you couldn't work with them, don't say so.

Don't burn your bridges. You never know when you might decide you actually do want to work for this company after all, or you may have to work with them or some of their staff in a different context, role or company. Always be nice.

'If you decide to decline a job offer, putting it in writing is also the best way.'

Handing in your notice

At the same time as you accept a new job offer, you have to hand in your notice at your current job, if you have one. If you are not working already then your new employer will probably want you to start as soon as possible.

If you already have a job, you will have to hand in your notice with your current employer and work out your notice period with them before you can start your new job. Your notice period should not be any longer than one week for every year you have worked with the company, up to a maximum of 12 weeks. However, the length of your notice period will depend on what it says in your current contract, so check that before agreeing a start date with your new employer.

It is a good idea not to hand in your notice with your current employer before you are officially offered a new job – even if you think your job interview went really well – because you may not get the job and you don't want to burn any bridges with your current employer or find yourself out of work if you don't get the new job you've applied for.

You might suddenly get a rush of nostalgia and feel sad about leaving your old job and your friends and colleagues, or you might be really relieved and excited to be moving on. Whatever your feelings, the same goes for handing in your notice as for accepting or rejecting a job offer: put it in writing and keep it short and polite.

Address it to your boss and also make a copy for your company's HR department, if it has one. Thank them for having you on their staff and explain that you have accepted the offer of a new job elsewhere and therefore you wish to resign and work out your notice period. Also say whether you want to take any holiday that you have outstanding before you leave, or if you would prefer to be paid for any days of annual leave that you haven't used.

Set up a meeting with your boss or line manager so you can tell them in person that you wish to hand in your notice, and give them the letter, as well as any copies that you have for the HR department. Don't just leave it on your boss's desk or post it to them without any explanation.

If your company doesn't want to lose you then they may try to get you to stay by offering you more money or a promotion. Be prepared for this to happen. If you are determined to leave and move on to your new job, make this clear and stick to your guns. Besides, if you are that indispensible then surely they should have promoted or rewarded you before now. However, if you really want to stay or are tempted by their offer then consider it, but be warned – turning down the new job offer if you have already accepted it will not go down well with your new company.

Your current employer may also ask you to take part in an 'exit interview', so they can get an idea of why you are leaving, what you thought of your time at the company, agree on your leaving date and so on. Once again, be polite and don't burn your bridges.

On rare occasions, if your current employer is concerned that your job entails you having access to information – such as contacts or sales leads – that could be beneficial to your new employer, they may accept your resignation and ask you to leave without working through any notice period.

When you do leave, don't get emotional and, if you didn't like working there, resist the temptation to tell everyone what you thought of them. Be professional at all times.

Summing Up

- Get the job offer and your contract in writing.

- Don't let yourself be rushed into accepting or rejecting it.

- Read the contract carefully and seek advice if you have any queries.

- Be brave – negotiate on the salary or other terms if they are not what you expected.

- Be realistic and be prepared to compromise if you really want the job.

- Know your rights when it comes to the minimum wage, SSP and annual leave.

- Make sure you are totally happy before you sign your contract and accept the job.

- Accept or reject all job offers in writing.

- Meet your boss to hand in your notice in person, and give them a written letter confirming your intentions.

- Always be polite, and don't burn your bridges.

Chapter Six

Dealing with Rejection

So you've had your interview and you felt it all went well, but then you get the letter telling you that you haven't got the job; or perhaps it's been two weeks since your interview and you still haven't heard.

If you are still waiting for a decision a couple of weeks after your interview, get on the phone and try to speak to the person you met, or the company's HR department, to see what the news is. It could just be that they are taking a long time to decide on who gets the job, or it might be that they simply haven't got around to writing to you with a 'no'. Either way, by taking the initiative and getting in touch with them, at least you'll know where you stand.

Alternatively, if you've received a rejection letter then it can be a big disappointment, especially if you thought you had done really well in your interview.

While you may not have got the job, all is not lost. There is a lot you can learn from this experience if you handle it in the right way.

Ask for feedback

The first thing to do is to get in touch with the HR department or the person who interviewed you and ask for some feedback about why they chose another candidate over you.

If you're lucky, they should be willing to give you some useful information about why they decided not to choose you for the job.

'If you are still waiting for a decision a couple of weeks after your interview, get on the phone and try to speak to the person who you met, or the company's HR department, to see what the news is.'

The best sort of rejection to hear is that they found someone more qualified for the position than you were. In this case, you know that you did your best but there was simply someone else who fitted the bill better than you. There's not much you can learn from this, apart from asking where your skills or experience had gaps compared with the person they chose.

Alternatively, they might say that you weren't well enough prepared for the interview, didn't seem to know enough about the company or the job in question, or didn't have the skills they wanted for the job. In this case, these are obvious weaknesses that you can work on for future interviews.

Learn from your mistakes

If your feedback showed you that you'd let yourself down in the interview by not being prepared enough, or if you simply feel that you fluffed your chance in some way or another, learn from your mistakes and make sure it doesn't happen again.

If it was particular skills that you were lacking, is there any way you can add these to your CV? Do you need some extra qualifications in order to successfully get a job in the field you are interested in? Perhaps it was something as simple as getting lost on your way to the interview and being late. There is probably quite a lot you can do next time to improve your chances.

Have another look at the interview tips and techniques that we covered in chapter 4. Practice makes perfect, and no one is ever perfect, so it pays to never stop practising.

Are there any other jobs there?

Once you've got some feedback – and unless you totally disgraced yourself at the interview – ask the person you are talking to whether there are any other vacancies with their organisation that you could apply for.

Occasionally, some employers specify in their job advertisements that previously unsuccessful applicants need not apply for other roles at the same company. However, on the whole, if you made a good impression at your interview but simply weren't suitably qualified for that particular job, most companies will generally consider you for another position.

Ask to be kept on file

If you have received a rejection letter then it may well say that the company will automatically keep your details on file in case another suitable position comes up.

Sometimes this is just their way of trying to soften the blow of not offering you the job, but some companies really do hang on to your details and, if they liked you at interview, may well get in touch when positions arise which are more suited to your skills.

If you really liked the idea of working for a particular company, but didn't get the job you applied for, it is worth calling them and asking for your details to be kept on file. Being proactive – but not pushy – always creates a good impression. You never know, your persistence may well pay off.

Volunteer/intern

If you really had your heart set on working for a specific company but didn't get the job you wanted, something else you can do is to ask if they will take you on for some work experience or an internship.

As well as helping you add to your skills and get exactly the kind of experience they are looking for, it also shows that you are keen and willing to learn. Another bonus of volunteering or interning is that you will get some great contacts, and it is an ideal way for you to see if you like the company as much from the inside as you did from the outside.

'If you really liked the idea of working for a particular company, but didn't get the job you applied for, it is worth calling them and asking for your details to be kept on file.'

Keep in touch

If there are no other positions on offer and the company doesn't have any intern vacancies either, the next best thing you can do is to keep in touch with them. Give their HR department, hiring manager or the person you met at your interview a call every month or so, or send them an email. Let them know that you are still interested in working for them, and also tell them a bit about what you've been up to. This way, you can update them on any new skills you've picked up since they interviewed you. By letting them know you would still like to be part of their team, you will keep yourself in the front of their minds when they come to hiring again.

Keep networking

'Tell everyone you know that you are looking for a job, and what kind of industry you want to work in.'

The chances are that there is more than one company doing the kind of work you are interested in, and so it follows that there will be other job vacancies elsewhere that you might also be interested in.

Tell everyone you know that you are looking for a job, and what kind of industry you want to work in. There is a theory – called six degrees of separation – that everyone in the world is connected to everyone else through only six steps. This means that you probably know someone who knows someone else who knows other people who are looking to hire someone just like you.

We've talked about the fact before that not every single job vacancy is widely advertised, and sometimes word of mouth is how you will come across a position. Tell people you meet at school or college, at work, at parties, on Twitter or Facebook – anywhere you interact and meet other people. By spreading the word about what you are after, you increase your chances of finding the kind of job you want.

Maintain your momentum

Don't let rejections knock you back. If the employer has decided you are not right for the job then you probably would have struggled to do it, wouldn't have fitted in and would have felt miserable.

The thing to do is to keep trying and not get too disheartened. Ask them for feedback, keep in touch if you still really want to work there, and keep looking for the next job opportunity. If you stay focused on your search then something will come up, and it will most probably be an even better job than the ones you didn't get before.

What to do if you think you've been discriminated against

If you think you didn't get the job because you were being discriminated against because of your gender, disability, race, nationality, age or any other reason, then you might have the right to make a claim against the person or company in question.

We will talk in more detail about discrimination in chapter 10, but one of the first things you can do is to contact your local Citizens Advice Bureau for more information and advice.

Summing Up

- Everyone is turned down for a job they want at some time or another – don't get too disheartened.

- Ask the company for feedback about why they decided not to give you the job.

- Learn from any mistakes you might have made so you don't repeat them.

- Brush up on your interview technique if necessary.

- Add to your skills and fill any gaps with extra training or qualifications.

- Ask for your details to be kept on file in case any similar vacancies come up.

- Consider volunteering or interning to get more experience.

- Be proactive, and keep in touch with companies you really want to work for.

- Tell everyone you know to tell everyone they know that you are looking for work.

- Don't give up, stay focused and keep applying – something will come up.

'Everyone is turned down for a job they want at some time or another – don't get too disheartened.'

Chapter Seven

Applying for Your First Job

Applying for your very first job straight after leaving school, college or university can seem like a difficult task. Many job advertisements say they are looking for people with some level of experience, but if you've never had a job before then you aren't going to have much, if any.

It's feels like a vicious circle – if no one gives you a job then you won't have any experience, but if you haven't got any experience then no one will give you a job.

Don't be put off. Yes, lack of experience is a hurdle, but it's only a minor one. Prospective employers will know from your age that you won't have all the experience and skills they are looking for, and they will bear this in mind.

Your task is to show them what skills and experience you do have that could also be useful in the job they are looking to fill. The best way to do this is to read through the job application very carefully and pick out all the words they use to describe the type of person they are looking for – such as 'a good communicator', 'computer literate', 'a team player' – and make sure that your CV and covering letter or application form for the job clearly mention your skills in all those areas.

As well as pointing out the formal, educational qualifications you have gained, think of activities you have taken part in and skills you have learned which will show you in the best light.

- Have you been part of a sports team?
- Have you been a member of a band or orchestra?
- Have you taken part in Duke of Edinburgh awards?

'Applying for your very first job straight after leaving school, college or university can seem like a difficult task.'

- Have you been a Guide or a Scout?
- Have you done any work experience placements?
- Have you passed your driving test?
- Have you learnt to speak another language?

Things like these show that you have taken part in activities outside of education and broadened your horizons and experience in other ways. These kinds of extra-curricular skills also show that you have other qualities that employers are looking for, such as being a team player, being motivated and organised.

Using careers centres

Your school, college or university may well operate a careers advice service, so make use of it as much as you can to find out about the different job and training options which are open to you.

Depending on what qualifications you have, careers advisers can help you match these up with your other skills and interests and help you decide what possible career paths are open to you.

Careers advice centres can also help you with writing your CV, provide Internet access so that you can search and apply for jobs online, and give you advice about going to interviews.

Connexions

If there isn't a careers advice service or officer at your school or college, and you live in England, then you could have a chat with your local Connexions service.

Connexions began in 2001 as a service offering all kinds of advice to 13-19-year-olds living in England, as well as for young people up to age 25 who have disabilities or learning difficulties.

It is a good place to start if you are looking for some career advice. You can find out more by visiting the Connexions website, calling the helpline or finding your local Connexions service office (see help list). All calls to Connexions Direct are free from a landline, and an adviser will ring you back on your mobile.

The government has a useful website at http://careersadvice.direct.gov.uk. There is also the government's nextstep scheme, which offers careers advice to those aged 20 and over, or those aged 18 or 19 if they have been referred by Jobcentre Plus.

If you live in Scotland then visit www.careers-scotland.org.uk. If you are in Wales, have a look at www.careerswales.com. If you are in Northern Ireland, try www.careersserviceni.com for more advice.

Apprenticeships

If you like the idea of learning and earning money at the same time then an apprenticeship could be the right option for you.

It can take up to four years to complete an apprenticeship but at the end you will have gained a nationally recognised qualification, learned news skills and have a job.

Government guidelines require you to be aged at least 16 to start an apprenticeship and, depending your grades in GCSE maths and English, you may have to take a literacy and numeracy test.

There are three levels of apprenticeship available:

- Apprenticeships (equivalent to five good GCSE passes).
- Advanced Apprenticeships (equivalent to two A level passes).
- Higher Apprenticeships (lead to qualifications at NVQ Level 4 or even a foundation degree).

As an apprentice you can expect to get paid at least £95 a week – although research suggests that the average apprentice takes home around £170 per week – and the government or your employer pays for your training, not you. You can also expect at least 20 days' paid holiday per year, as well as bank holidays, just like an ordinary employee.

Apprenticeships (and Advanced Apprenticeships) can lead to:

- A National Vocational Qualification (NVQ) at Level 2 or Level 3.

'If you like the idea of learning and earning money at the same time then an apprenticeship could be the right option for you.'

- A Key Skills qualification – such as problem-solving and using technology; or a technical certificate – such as a BTEC or City & Guilds Progression Award.

- Other qualifications needed for particular occupations.

Not every industry sector offers apprenticeships, but you can find out more or search and apply for apprenticeship vacancies in England on the national apprenticeships website. See the help list for information on apprenticeships in Northern Ireland, Scotland and Wales.

Entry to Employment

If you are aged between 16 and 18 and live in England, you could try an Entry to Employment (e2e) programme if you're not ready to go straight into an apprenticeship, employment with training or further education.

With e2e you can try out different work and learning situations in order to help you decide what kind of apprenticeship, training or job you would like to do. You have to commit to between 16-40 hours a week to courses covering basic and key skills, vocational training and personal and social development – which are aimed at developing your motivation, confidence and workplace skills – known as 'Key Skills' and 'Skills for Life'.

If you take part in an e2e programme, you can also apply for an Education Maintenance Allowance (EMA) of £30 a week. You can find out more at the Directgov website – search for 'education maintenance allowance' from the homepage (see help list).

Benefits for young job seekers

Everyone can find it hard to make ends meet financially while looking for a job. If you're 16 or over you might be entitled to claim certain benefits or tax credits from the government payments while you are looking for work.

Exactly what kind of benefits and how much you could claim depend on various factors including your age, but your local Jobcentre Plus office will be able to tell you more about the different types of benefit available to you, and help you fill in a claim form.

The government information website www.direct.gov.uk has plenty of information about the main types of benefit:

- Income Support – for those over 16 and unable to work because they are a lone parent, an at-home parent looking after their children, registered as a disabled person, or responsible for the care of a relative who is disabled.

- Jobseeker's Allowance – for those over 18 who are unemployed, not in education and looking for work. You could also be eligible if you have a job where you work less than 16 hours every week. If you're 16 or 17, you may be eligible for Jobseeker's Allowance in exceptional circumstances, such as estrangement from your family.

- Housing Benefit – to help pay your rent if your income and savings are below a certain level and you are living with people other than your relatives.

- Working Tax Credit – mainly for people over 25, but if you're aged 16 or over and have children or a disability that affects your ability to work or look for work, you may also be able to claim.

Volunteering

Volunteering some of your time to help out at charities and community projects is a great way to add to your skills, try out different types of work and boost your CV before you leave education, after you've left and are looking for your first job, and even once you've found a job.

You won't get paid for what you do, but volunteering projects across the UK are always on the look out for people to lend a hand, and will be extremely grateful for any help you can offer.

Whatever kind of job you think you want to do, you can probably find a volunteer opportunity that matches it somehow. For example, if you want to work with children then you could volunteer at your local playgroup. Maybe you are interested in working in accountancy or public relations? Any medium to

'Volunteering some of your time to help out at charities and community projects is a great way to add to your skills, try out different types of work and boost your CV before you leave education, after you've left and are looking for your first job, and even once you've found a job.'

large charity organisation will have a person or a department which does that kind of work, and they may well love to have someone volunteering a few hours a week to help them out. Even if you end up filing or making the tea, you will get an insider's view of how those jobs work, and make some good contacts – and possibly even friends – while you do it.

If you can't find somewhere to volunteer yourself, there are lots of different volunteering organisations that can point you in the right direction.

Volunteering England (see help list) has information about how to volunteer, as well as organisations which are looking for volunteers.

Another volunteering charity is V (see help list), which has been set up to promote youth volunteering in England and is hoping to encourage one million more 16-25 year olds to volunteer their free time to help out on projects in their local area.

If you're prepared to live away from home then how about full-time volunteering through organisations such as Community Service Volunteers (see help list), which will find you a placement for between four and 12 months, and you'll also get an allowance, and free accommodation and food.

Volunteering is an excellent way to give something back to the community and boost your confidence in a working environment at the same time. If you do a good job then you can always ask for a reference when you leave, which will come in useful in your future job hunting. You've got nothing to lose, except your inexperience.

Summing Up

- Don't be put off by your lack of experience – employers will expect that from first-time job hunters.

- Make sure your CV and covering letter or application form mention the skills you have which match the job description.

- Mention activities and skills you have developed outside of formal education.

- Make use of careers advice centres as much as possible.

- Apprenticeships give you skills and qualifications, as well as a wage while you learn and work.

- Talk to your local Jobcentre Plus about any benefits you might be entitled to whilst you look for work.

- Consider volunteering to build up your skills, confidence and contacts.

'Make sure your CV and covering letter or application form mention the skills you have which match the job description.'

Chapter Eight

Returning to Work After a Break

Going back to work after any considerable period of time off is bound to feel like a challenge.

People have breaks from working for many reasons:

- Some because they choose to – such as taking a sabbatical or a long holiday.

- Some are out of their control – such as being made redundant.

- Some for other reasons – such as maternity leave, long-term sickness leave, or simply rejoining the workforce after a long period not working.

If the break was your choice

If you've been away from work because you chose to have a sabbatical or extended holiday then it's more than likely that your employer agreed to your break and you are returning to your old job.

Depending on how long you've been away, you might be excited, relieved or even daunted by the prospect of returning to work.

If you are returning to your old job, be prepared that there could have been changes in the technology, people and skills you were familiar with before you went away.

'Going back to work after any considerable period of time off is bound to feel like a challenge.'

Your own attitude to work, and the attitude of your colleagues towards you, could also be different. It is possible that some people may think you are not career-minded because you have taken a break, so be prepared to explain how what you have learned and achieved during your time away can add value to your working life.

If you are looking for a new job, rather than returning to your old job, then be prepared to explain to potential employers how you have used your time off productively, and what you have learnt.

Remember that nowadays many employers are more used to people taking sabbaticals and time out for other things, so aim to put a positive spin on what you have been doing during your break and make yourself sound like a flexible and go-getting individual who would be a credit to any organisation.

However, do be prepared for some reverse culture shock of your own. No matter how used to it you were before, you are not going to be able to snap back into your old nine-to-five routine immediately.

'Be nice to yourself, and be clear with your boss about any training or induction that you feel would make it easier for you to get back up-to-date with your working practices.'

Be nice to yourself, and be clear with your boss about any training or induction that you feel would make it easier for you to get back up-to-date with your working practices. Technology, office systems and ways of working will have undoubtedly moved on during your time away. Also bear in mind that former colleagues may have moved roles or been promoted in your absence, and treat them accordingly.

If the break was not of your choosing

In difficult economic times such as the ones we have experienced lately, many people have been made redundant and the number of job vacancies has contracted.

If you are looking for work, it may take you longer than you had expected to find a new job, and it's easy to get disheartened, but don't be put off. Even if you have been out of work for many months, employers know that these are not the easiest of times for people looking for work, and as long as you can show that you have been using your time productively while you have been unemployed then they shouldn't hold this against you.

Studying, working part time, volunteering, interning and doing work experience – no matter what your age – are all good ways to make use of your spare time while out of work and job-hunting, and will add to your experience and boost the transferable skills that employers are looking for.

If you were sacked

You don't have to come straight out and tell prospective employers if you were sacked from you last job. However, if they ask you, it is better not to lie about it because they will probably find out from your previous employer when they ask them for a reference for you.

There are other ways of phrasing it when it comes to explaining why you left your last job. Instead of simply saying 'I was fired', you could say 'The job wasn't really working out for me so my boss and I decided I should explore other options' or 'It became clear that my strengths are in other areas and so I left by mutual agreement'. The person doing the hiring will know what you are talking about, but this makes a more pleasant way of explaining it.

Going back to your old job after maternity leave

When you return to work after ordinary maternity leave (the first 26 weeks of your statutory maternity leave), you have a right to the same job and the same terms and conditions as if you hadn't been absent.

This is also the case if you take additional leave (the last 26 weeks of your statutory maternity leave), although this doesn't apply if your employer can prove it is not reasonably practical for you to return to your original job (for example, because the job no longer exists). If this happens, you must be offered alternative work with the same terms and conditions as if you hadn't been absent.

If you take the full 52 weeks' statutory maternity leave then you don't need to give notice that you're coming back, but it's a good idea to do so. If you wish to return earlier, for example, when your statutory maternity pay ends, you must give at least eight weeks' notice.

If you decide not to return to work at all, you must give your employer notice in the normal way according to what your contract says.

Returning to work after illness

If you have been off work with illness or injury for more than a month, then this is considered a long-term absence.

Returning to work after such a time away might seem like an uphill struggle, but if you are fit and able to get back to your job then the sooner you return, the better it will be for your emotional and physical health.

If you have been off work because of an injury, illness or accident that has left you with a disability, then your employer has a duty under the Disability Discrimination Act 1995 to make reasonable adjustments – such as ensuring there is wheelchair access, for example – so that you can continue to do your job.

Your employer should have kept in touch with you during your period of absence from work. Therefore, if your illness or injury means that it is impossible for you to do exactly the same job as before, the Disability Discrimination Act requires them to make adjustments to provide you with alternative work where possible.

If you feel you are being discriminated against in any way to do with your return to work, speak to the Citizens Advice Bureau, or your union representative if you have one.

Rejoining the workforce after a long period away

If you have spent any considerable amount of time away from the world of work for whatever reasons, then re-entering the workforce – either into your old job or with a new one – is bound to be at least a little unsettling.

You may find that your ambitions, priorities and goals have shifted during your time away from work, so don't rush in to getting a job. Take the time to carefully consider how your skills and experience match up with your expectations of the sort of work you want to do.

Again, as long as you can explain your absence – perhaps you were a full-time carer, or had an income which made it possible for you not to need to work – and can show that you have continued to develop and use skills that make you a good candidate as a prospective employee, your time away from work should not put you at a disadvantage when looking for a job.

If you think you could do with brushing up on some skills before you relaunch yourself into the job market – for example, computer skills – then talk to your local Jobcentre Plus to see what advice or training they can offer or recommend. You could consider volunteering or working part time in the field you want to get in to, in order to add to your experience and confidence.

Remember, it's never too late to do the kind of job you are interested in, but be positive about the time you have taken out from work.

'Take the time to carefully consider how your skills and experience match up with your expectations of the sort of work you want to do.'

Summing Up

- Be ready to explain why you have had a break from work.

- Make sure you can demonstrate what skills and experience you have gained during your time away from the workforce.

- Don't lie if you are asked whether you were sacked, but don't volunteer the information if interviewers don't bring it up themselves.

- Keep in touch with your employer if you are on maternity or sick leave.

- If you feel you are being discriminated against, talk to your local Citizens Advice Bureau, or your union representative if you have one.

- Consider volunteering or working part time to get more experience in the field you are interested in.

- Talk to your local Jobcentre Plus about any top-up training they might offer or recommend.

- Be positive about your return to work.

Chapter Nine

Choosing a New Career

Many people find themselves changing direction during the course of their careers for many reasons including redundancy, relocating or because they like the idea of doing something different.

There are also plenty of people who would really like to change where their career path is heading, but don't know how to go about it or are concerned about how much it will cost them.

To change, or not to change?

If you find yourself in a position where you are considering a career change, it is important to really think about your motivation behind it.

Is it really a new career you want, or just a new job doing what you already do but somewhere else? Take a close look at what is making you feel that way. Perhaps you feel stuck in a rut with your current job, or you don't like the people you work with? Maybe you fell into the line of work you do now, but have never really been that fond of it?

Money is not the only thing that motivates people to go to work; you need to be getting a bit more out of your nine-to-five than simply using it to pay the bills. If nothing about your job excites you or you spend every Sunday evening dreading the arrival of Monday, then perhaps you need to rethink what you are doing.

Not everyone jumps out of bed in the morning full of excitement at the prospect of going to work, but if you don't at least like what you do during working hours then it could be time for a change.

'Many people find themselves changing direction during the course of their careers for many reasons including redundancy, relocating or because they like the idea of doing something different.'

Dealing with change

Change is a scary concept for most people and if you've spent your whole career in one industry or field, or trained for a specific job, then feeling like you want to do something different can be a terrifying prospect and one that you might not want to even admit to yourself.

The thing to remember is that if you really, really want to do it, it can be done – although it will probably need you to make some sacrifices and adjustments along the way.

Take your time… but don't procrastinate

'An important first stage of changing career direction is to do your research. There's nothing to be gained by rushing into change.'

An important first stage of changing career direction is to do your research. There's nothing to be gained by rushing into change, and if you spend a bit of time carefully planning your next move and how you are going to go about it, it will really pay off.

Having said that, don't procrastinate. Lots of people put off going after the job of their dreams until their children have left home, their mortgage is paid off, they're a bit older or other such excuses. None of these are proper reasons for delaying doing what they really want to do. In fact, the real reason is probably quite simply that they are afraid.

Careers advice

A good place to start if you need help with choosing your next career step is your local Careers Advice Direct (see help list). They will be able to give you free, impartial advice, and talking to one of their advisers is a good way to make things a bit clearer in your own mind.

Another useful exercise, which can help you focus on the kind of industry you might want to work in, is to look at some 'career profiles'. These tell you the skills and qualifications you need for particular jobs, and you can find more about them at the Alliance of Sector Skills Councils website.

The government's nextstep service also offers free advice on training, learning and employment, and if you are thinking of changing careers its advisers can help you identify the new skills you'll need. You can also get advice on showing employers that what you've learnt in one job can be valuable in another – what are known as 'transferable skills'.

You can use the nextstep service if you are aged 20 or over, or aged 18 or 19, and have been referred to nextstep by Jobcentre Plus.

Starting at the bottom

Let's say you've trained and worked as a nurse, but then you decide you want to be a meteorologist. It's not something that's going to happen overnight. You may well have some transferable skills, but the simple fact is that the most realistic way you are going to be able to make this change happen is by starting again.

Whatever kind of career you want to get into, it is probably going to mean that you will have to do some retraining. This could be anything from a university course to doing an apprenticeship, or simply finding a company that does what you want to do and starting at the bottom and working your way up.

'Whatever kind of career you want to get into, it is probably going to mean that you will have to do some retraining.'

Further education

If simply starting at the bottom isn't an option, you might have to consider taking some time out to retrain for your new career.

We've talked about apprenticeships in chapter 7, but training or retraining could also include going back to university or college to add to your skills. The Universities and Colleges Admissions Service (UCAS) website enables you to search for courses at universities and colleges in the UK, apply for them online and track the progress of your application (see help list for details).

Funding further learning

If you are set on a change of direction and discover you really need some extra qualifications in order to do the kind of work you want to do, don't be put off by the cost implications of further learning.

Some courses are free to do – including many literacy and numeracy courses, and those which lead to your first qualification equivalent to GCSEs and A Levels – and you may be entitled to financial help towards the costs of others, as well as related costs such as travel and childcare, depending on your personal circumstances.

Careers Advice and nextstep advisers can tell you about any money you could get to help pay for your learning, such as loans, grants or bursaries. Loans, of course, have to be repaid. Grants – although they are rarely large enough to support you financially – are a useful addition that you don't have to pay back. Bursaries are granted by the universities or colleges themselves, or even by a company if they are linked to a particular career.

Some possible sources of funding that you might be entitled to are listed below.

Professional and Career Development Loans

A Professional and Career Development Loan could help you pay for vocational or work-related learning. It's a deferred repayment bank loan which allows you to borrow between £300 and £10,000, so you'll have to pay it back once you've left your course. However, you don't pay interest for the period when you're in learning.

Adult Learning Grant

The Adult Learning Grant (ALG) could give you up to £30 a week while you take your first full Level 2 or Level 3 qualification. You can use ALG to study for a range of qualifications including BTECs, NVQs, GSCEs and A Levels.

University or college grants

If you're considering a university or college course in the UK, the UCAS website has a comprehensive guide to finance at www.ucas.com/students/studentfinance which sets out what funding may be available to you.

Other grants and bursaries

There are other grants and bursaries available to help with learning costs.

The Residential Support Scheme offers accommodation costs if you need to study away from home. If you qualify, the scheme will help pay for your term-time accommodation. You may be able to claim up to £3,458 (£4,079 in the London area) towards your costs each year, up to a maximum of three years, depending on your household income.

If you're starting a new job at 50 or over, you may be able to get help with work-related training costs through the Fifty Plus In-work Training Grant. As with all grants, you'll need to meet certain conditions in order to qualify, but if you do then the grant could give you up to £1,500 towards work-related training, whether it's delivered by your employer, at a local college or through another learning provider. This can include tuition fees, books and course-related costs such as registration and exam fees.

You might also qualify for an educational grant from a charity trust. The Directory of Social Change's Grants for Individuals website (see help list) contains details of over 3,500 trusts operating nationally and locally which give at least £500 a year to individuals for welfare and educational purposes. Awards include £10 food vouchers made at Christmas and larger contributions such as grants for domestic items – for example, washing machines, wheelchairs and house adaptations.

Discretionary Support Funds

Colleges and school sixth forms can provide extra financial help through their Discretionary Support Funds, which are prioritised for those who face financial hardship. These funds can be used to help with:

- Financial hardship and emergencies.

- Childcare costs (for Ofsted-registered childcare).

- Accommodation costs for those who have to study further than the maximum distance from home.

- Essential course-related equipment, materials and field trips.

- Travel costs (for over 18s).

Volunteering and interning

We have already talked about volunteering and interning and their benefits in previous chapters, but it is worth mentioning again in the context of changing careers.

It is very likely that there will be a charity or business that operates in the area that you would like to work in. By spending some time volunteering or interning with them before you take the plunge into working in that particular field full time, you will learn a lot, add to your skills and meet people who do the kind of work you want to do.

Again, you probably won't get to do any of the big, exciting and important parts of the job, but you will experience the industry from the inside and get some great contacts which may well help you in your future job hunting.

Networking

Talking of contacts, networking is all about building up your connections as well as letting them all know what you can do and what it is you want to do in future.

- Talk to everyone you know and tell them you're on the hunt for a job. Ask them to also tell their friends, family and colleagues about you, and give them your phone number or email address so they can get in touch if anything comes up.

- Have some simple business cards printed with your name and contact details (lots of websites and printers can do this for a very reasonable price) so you can hand them out to people who you want to keep in contact with.

- Go to conferences and industry shows for the sector you want to work in. These are a great way to meet and chat to people, and learn more about the kind of career you want to pursue.

- Take advantage of the reach of social and professional networking websites such as Facebook, Twitter and LinkedIn.

By getting to know as many people as possible – both in the industry you want to work in, and beyond – you are increasing your chances of hearing about job vacancies and getting the sort of job you really want.

Explaining yourself

It is not a crime to want to change direction with your career, although many people will try to put you off starting again and might even give you a hard time about it.

There are lots of reasons for wanting to do something different – from redundancy to boredom or wanting a new challenge – and none of these mean you have 'failed' at what you did before. If you are going for interviews or applying for courses in a new field, you will have to be prepared to explain why you have decided to do something different.

The key is to sound proactive and engaged, rather than indecisive and negative when you talk about changing tack. Emphasising your transferrable skills is a good starting point when you need to convince someone of your suitability for a new career. There will be many skills that you have built up in your previous employment or educational history that will be relevant to your new chosen profession, so make sure you point these out.

Showing your enthusiasm for change is also important. If you can convince employers or course leaders that you are driven and committed to your proposed change of direction and that nothing is going to stop you from achieving your new goal, they will be more interested in having you on board.

'When you are looking for work, advice or work experience, talk to everyone you know and tell them that you are on the hunt for a job or would like to chat to someone who already does the kind of work you want to do.'

Summing Up

- Are you sure it's a new career you want, rather than just a new job?

- Take the time to carefully research and think about what you want to do.

- Don't be put off by the practical or financial implications of changing direction.

- Get plenty of advice – talk to professional career advisers, experts in the field you want to go into, friends and family.

- Be prepared to start at the bottom.

- Find out about courses or further training that could help.

- Look into the financial help that may be available to you. This could make all the difference.

- Try volunteering or interning to see if it's really the right career for you.

- Get networking, and tell everyone what you want to do.

- Be prepared to stand up for yourself and explain, with conviction, why you want a change in career.

- Read *Applying to University – The Essential Guide* by Anne Coates (Need2Know) for further guidance on the university process.

Chapter Ten

Discrimination and Your Rights

Equal opportunity laws exist in the UK to protect workers from all kinds of discrimination whilst at work, and also during the recruiting process. The basis of these laws is that people are treated equally and are employed, paid, trained and promoted only because of their skills, abilities and how they do their job, rather than because of any other factor.

Types of discrimination

According to UK law, you can't be discriminated against because of your:

- Gender.
- Marriage or civil partnership.
- Gender reassignment.
- Pregnancy and maternity leave.
- Sexual orientation.
- Disability.
- Race.
- Colour.
- Ethnic background.
- Nationality.
- Religion or belief.

'Equal opportunity laws exist in the UK to protect workers from all kinds of discrimination whilst at work, and also during the recruiting process.'

- Age.

Your employer also can't dismiss you or treat you less favourably than other workers because you:

- Work part time.
- Are on a fixed-term contract.

What is discrimination?

When it comes to applying for a job, discrimination happens when a prospective employer favours one candidate over another because of any of the reasons listed above.

So, for example, it is discrimination to offer a job to a younger candidate rather than one who is older but has the same skills on the basis of their ages alone. It is discrimination to decide to employ someone simply because they are white, rather than selecting another candidate who is just as able to do the job but comes from a minority ethnic community.

The recruitment process

It is also possible to be discriminated against during the recruitment process itself. For example, it would be discrimination to require a blind person to complete a written application form, or for an employer to insist that all interviewees have to climb several flights of stairs to attend the interview.

Fair testing

All tests for job applicants must be conducted in a non-discriminatory way, with alternative testing methods made available for people who cannot, for whatever reason, complete the tests in their original format.

For example, a written English test would discriminate against those whose first language is not English, although employers could justify it if having good written English was necessary for the particular role.

By law, employers have to make reasonable adjustments to modify a test for an applicant with a disability if they would otherwise be substantially disadvantaged compared with a non-disabled person. For example, by providing the test in a format they can use, or allowing them to bring a helper into the test with them.

When it's not discrimination

In some circumstances it is possible for employers to state that the ideal person to fill a role must be of a particular sex, race, religion/belief, age or sexual orientation and so on, because this is a genuine occupational qualification or requirement for the job.

For example, it may be possible to state that being:

- A fluent speaker of French is a requirement for a job as a French translator.
- A woman is a qualification for a job as an attendant in a women's public lavatory.
- A Muslim is necessary for a job with a Muslim charity.
- Heterosexual is a requirement for a job with a religious organisation whose religious believers object to homosexual practices.
- Aged under 20 is a requirement for a job as an actor playing the part of someone who is a teenager.

What to do if you've been discriminated against

The Directgov website has a letter template that you can fill in and send to the person or organisation you think has discriminated against you. The reply you get should help you decide how to handle the problem – for instance, whether you want to take the matter further and put a case to an employment tribunal.

Go to the Directgov website and search for 'making a complaint about discrimination' to find out more and download the template. You could also talk to your local Citizens Advice Bureau for advice about your rights and how to proceed.

'By law, employers have to make reasonable adjustments to modify a test for an applicant with a disability if they would otherwise be substantially disadvantaged compared with a non-disabled person.'

Employment tribunals

Employers must always be able to justify why they decided to hire a particular person, because if you believe that you have been unlawfully discriminated against during the recruitment process then you could take your case to an employment tribunal.

Let's take age discrimination as an example. Say you are in your forties and have not been offered a particular job you were interviewed for. During the interview process you felt that the interviewer made derogatory comments related to your age and how this would affect your ability to do the job in question. You have also found out that the person they ended up offering the job to is younger than you, but also less well qualified. In an instance such as this, you may well have a case to bring against the employer for age discrimination, although it is always possible that the successful candidate was chosen because they were, in more ways than you, more suitable for the position.

'Employers must always be able to justify why they decided to hire a particular person.'

If you truly believe you weren't selected for a particular job as a result of discriminatory practices, you can take your case to an employment tribunal, even though you are not an employee of the company in question. Again, your local Citizens Advice Bureau will be able to give you more advice about how to proceed.

Summing Up

- Equal opportunity laws protect workers from discrimination whilst at work and during the recruiting process.

- People must be employed only on the basis of their skills, abilities and how they do their job, rather than any other factor.

- Employers must always be able to justify why they decided to hire a particular person.

- All tests for job applicants must be conducted in a non-discriminatory way.

- Sometimes, what appears to be discrimination is actually a genuine occupational qualification or requirement for the job.

- If you believe that you have been unlawfully discriminated against during the recruitment process, you could take your case to an employment tribunal.

- Directgov and your local Citizens Advice Bureau have plenty of advice on this subject.

Help List

General information

Citizens Advice Bureau

www.citizensadvice.org.uk
A free, independent and confidential advice service which can help you resolve legal, financial and other problems. Use the search facility to find the telephone number of your local branch.

Connexions

Tel: 080 800 13 2 19
www.connexions-direct.com
Advice service for young people aged 13 to 19, living in England. It also provides support up to the age of 25 for young people who have learning difficulties or disabilities (or both).

Department for Work and Pensions (DWP)

Caxton House, Tothill Street, London, SW1H 9DA
www.dwp.gov.uk
Government department which oversees Jobcentre Plus, The Pensions Service and the Disability and Carers Service.

Directgov

www.direct.gov.uk
The UK government's digital service for people in England and Wales, with information and practical advice about public services. You can find information on the Disability Discrimination Act 1995 here.

Google

www.google.co.uk
The world's largest Internet search engine.

Jobcentre Plus

Tel: 08456 060 234 (job search helpline)
Tel: 0800 055 6688 (benefits helpline)
www.direct.gov.uk
An executive agency of the DWP which helps people of working age find jobs, as well as administering some benefits for people of working age. Jobcentre Plus has also launched an iPhone, iPod touch and iPad app which allows you to search through all the jobs held by Jobcentre Plus. You can download it for free from iTunes.

Royal Mail

www.royalmail.com
Royal Mail Group Ltd is the parent company of Royal Mail, the Post Office and Parcelforce Worldwide.

Careers advice

Alliance of Sector Skills Councils

www.sscalliance.org
The Alliance unites all 25 licensed UK Sector Skills Councils, which are the employer-driven organisations that give a voice to the employers of around 90% of the UK's workforce on skills issues. Search on this site to find out what skills you need to do certain jobs.

Careers Advice Direct

Tel: 0800 100 900
www.careersadvice.direct.gov.uk
Free and impartial careers advice for users in England and Wales.

Careers Advice Northern Ireland

www.careersserviceni.com
Free and impartial careers advice for users in Northern Ireland. Find information on apprenticeships in Northern Ireland by clicking on 'success through skills' and then entering the 'programmes' section.

Careers Scotland

www.careers-scotland.org.uk
Free and impartial careers advice for users in Scotland. Information on apprenticeships can be found by clicking 'education options', then 'training'.

Careers Wales

www.careerswales.com
Further free and impartial careers advice for users in Wales. The apprenticeships section is under '16 to 19 year olds', 'work and training' links.

Department for Employment and Learning (Northern Ireland)

www.delni.gov.uk
Find information on apprenticeships in Northern Ireland by clicking on 'success through skills' and then entering the 'programmes' section.

Entry to Employment (e2e)

www.connexions-direct.com
If you are aged 16-18, you live in England and are not participating in any form of post-16 learning, you can be admitted to the e2e work scheme if that is an appropriate option which will enable you to progress to an apprenticeship, further learning or a job. Click 'work' and then 'work schemes' for the details.

National apprenticeships

www.apprenticeships.org.uk
Search, view and apply for apprenticeships from across England.

nextstep

http://nextstep.direct.gov.uk

A free service that offers face-to-face help and advice on training, learning and the world of work. You can use nextstep if you are aged 20 or over, or aged 18 or 19 and you've been referred by Jobcentre Plus.

The Universities and Colleges Admissions Service (UCAS)

www.ucas.ac.uk

This is the organisation responsible for managing applications to higher education courses in the UK. Its website enables you to search for courses at universities and colleges, apply for them online and track the progress of your application.

Benefits, loans, grants and other funding

Adult Learning Grant

www.direct.gov.uk

The Adult Learning Grant (ALG) could give you up to £30 a week while you take your first full Level 2 or Level 3 qualification. You can use the ALG to study for a range of qualifications including BTECs, NVQs, GSCEs and A Levels. Search 'adult learning grant' from the Directgov homepage.

Care to Learn

Tel: 0800 121 8989 (helpline)

www.direct.gov.uk

Help with the cost of your childcare while you're learning, if you're under 20 and have one or more children. Search 'care to learn' from the Directgov homepage.

The Directory of Social Change's Grants for Individuals

www.grantsforindividuals.org.uk

Details of over 3,500 trusts operating nationally and locally which give at least £500 a year to individuals for welfare and educational purposes. Awards include £10 food vouchers made at Christmas and larger contributions such as grants for domestic items like washing machines, wheelchairs and house adaptations.

Discretionary Support Funds

www.direct.gov.uk

Colleges and school sixth forms can provide extra financial help through their Discretionary Support Funds, which are prioritised for those who face financial hardship. Search 'discretionary support funds' from the Directgov homepage.

Education Maintenance Allowance (EMA)

www.direct.gov.uk

The EMA is a payment of up to £30 a week in term time for people aged 16-18 in England, to help you carry on learning. If you live or study in Northern Ireland, Scotland or Wales, which have their own EMA schemes, you must apply to the EMA scheme for the country you intend to study in. Search 'education maintenance allowance' from the Directgov homepage.

Fifty Plus In-work Training Grant

www.direct.gov.uk

Offers help with work-related training costs to those starting a new job and aged 50 or over. If you meet certain conditions in order to qualify, the grant could give you up to £1,500 towards work-related training, tuition fees, books and other course-related costs like registration and exam fees. Search 'fifty plus in-work training grant' from the Directgov homepage.

Professional and Career Development Loans

www.direct.gov.uk

A Professional and Career Development Loan could help you pay for learning that enhances your job skills or career prospects. It's a bank loan, so you'll have to pay it back once you've finished your studies, but you don't pay interest while you're in learning. Search 'professional and career development loans' from the Directgov homepage.

The Residential Support Scheme

www.direct.gov.uk

This offers accommodation costs if you need to study away from home. If you qualify, the scheme will help pay for term-time accommodation and you may be able to claim up to £3,458 (£4,079 in the London area) towards costs each year, up to a maximum of three years, depending on your household income. Search 'residential support scheme' from the Directgov homepage.

University or college grants

www.ucas.com/students/studentfinance
If you're considering a university or college course, the UCAS website has a comprehensive guide to finance.

Social networking sites

Facebook

www.facebook.com
A social networking site where registered users can find and connect with other people also using the site.

FriendsReunited

www.friendsreunited.com
This site lets you find and keep in touch with school and college friends, as well as work colleagues.

LinkedIn

www.linkedin.com
LinkedIn is like Facebook, but it is used by professionals and has more of a work and career-orientated outlook.

Twitter

www.twitter.com
Twitter is another form of social networking site, where you can 'follow' other users and share your own tweets, which are 140-character statements about what you are doing and thinking.

Volunteering

Community Service Volunteers

www.csv.org.uk
A training and volunteering charity which involves over 150,000 volunteers every year in opportunities that help transform the lives of more than one million people across the UK.

V

http://vinspired.com
Vinspired connects 16 to 25-year-olds with volunteering opportunities in England.

Volunteering England

www.volunteering.org.uk
The national volunteering development agency for England.

VSO UK (Voluntary Service Overseas)

Carlton House, 27a Carlton Drive, Putney, London, SW15 2BS
Tel: 020 8780 7500
www.vso.org.uk
A leading independent international development organisation that works through volunteers to fight poverty in developing countries.